Unbelievable Freedom

How We Transformed Our Health and
Happiness with Intermittent Fasting

Ryan and Kim Smith

Dedication

To Gram B, whose spirit continues to guide us to enjoy life and to encourage others.

Lorraine Lillian Hewes Beatham, 1918-2013

Table of Contents

Foreword

Unbelievable Freedom!

Yes, those are powerful words. Intermittent fasting is a powerful lifestyle, after all.

When Kim and Ryan asked me to write the foreword for their book, I was both thrilled and honored. I have known Kim since 2017 when she waltzed into my Facebook intermittent fasting support group with her contagious smile. From the very beginning, Kim was a shining light within the group. Her positivity came through in every post that she made, and soon, other members began to look forward to her posts. We all loved seeing her progress photos! One thing was constant: as time went on, her eyes got bigger and bigger...and so did that smile. Many of her progress photos also included her husband, Ryan, and it was apparent that they were in it together.

As the months went by, Kim's enthusiasm for intermittent fasting grew...as she and Ryan both shrunk. I could tell that Kim was a leader and that her excitement was spreading to those within her community. I remember when she first reached out to me with the idea to start her own intermittent fasting support group so she could mentor her own friends. I had a hunch right then that Kim was going to impact more lives than she could fathom.

I loved watching her journey over the months. I remember when Kim was thrilled to fit into a size 10. I told her to prepare to be amazed, because her body was not done yet. Before we knew it, she was in a size 6. I told her she STILL wasn't done yet. I'm not sure if she believed me that day, but I was confident. Now, she is rocking a size 4. I am pretty sure that, like me, Kim never dreamed that she would be fitting into a size 4. When you are obese, a size 4 seems like a pipe dream.

I remember those days well. You see, I topped the scale at 210 pounds in April of 2014. My whole diet story is in my first book, *Delay, Don't Deny: Living an Intermittent Fasting Lifestyle*. On the fateful day, when my own obesity slapped me in the face, I was on a cruise with my family, and I couldn't believe that woman in the photos was actually me. Right then, I vowed that I would not be that woman any longer…the woman moving through life in an oversized body that didn't feel like it could possibly belong to me. I felt that if only I could get back into a size 10, I would be thrilled. A size 6 seemed too good to be true, but I put it on my vision board and began the search for some method that would allow me to shed my outer fat-suit; because that is what it felt like to me. Can anyone relate? I knew I was still inside there somewhere, but I needed to emerge. And, one way or another, I was going to make it happen.

Like Kim and Ryan, I took some missteps, twists, and turns along the way, but my journey finally led me to intermittent fasting. I was able to lose over 75 pounds (that has morphed into 80+ over time), and when I hit my initial goal weight of 135 pounds, I was amazed to find that I was not, after all, a size 6…I was actually a size FOUR. What?!?!?! In my wildest dreams, I never expected to be a size 4.

Now, a couple of years later, I am no longer a size 4. Why? You may be thinking that it must be some weight regain, right? After all, "nobody" can lose weight and keep it off. According to *The American Journal of Clinical Nutrition* (2005), only about 20% of dieters are able to lose even a measly 10% of their initial body weight and keep it off for over a year…and I lost about 38% of my initial body weight. So, I MUST have regained some or most of it, right?

No, it's true that I am no longer a size 4. I have to admit that it was a little sad to have to retire some of my beautiful "goal clothes" that I bought when I hit that magical size 4.

I had to retire my beautiful size 4 clothes because…are you ready for it? They became TOO LARGE. Yep. It's true. Over the three plus years that I have been in "maintenance" after losing 80+ pounds, I continued to lose clothing sizes without even trying. Now,

I don't even pick up size 4 clothes in the store, because I know they will be too big for me. I head straight to the end of the rack with the size 0s and size 2s. That's where I find my clothes these days.

Yes, intermittent fasting gives us *Unbelievable Freedom*. For the first time in my life, I don't worry that my I will gain weight and have to buy new, bigger clothes. For the first time in my life, I don't count calories, fat grams, carbs… I eat to satiety, and then I stop eating when I have had enough. For the first time in my life, I am *free* to eat foods that are delicious every day of my life.

For the first time in my life, I know that I am off of the diet roller coaster for good.

Unbelievable Freedom.

Are you ready to hear how Kim and Ryan found their own *Unbelievable Freedom*? Their heart-warming story lies ahead in the pages of this book. A lot within their story reminds me of myself, and I'm pretty sure that some or much of it will feel familiar to you, too. All the years of struggle. The "giving up." (I did that, too, for a while.) But, just like Kim and Ryan, we only have to try ONE MORE TIME than we quit in order to be successful. Intermittent fasting is here for you when you are ready, just like it was here for me and it was here for Kim and Ryan.

Unbelievable Freedom. Kim and Ryan have found it, and their story is inspiring.

Unbelievable Freedom. It's waiting for you, too.

Gin Stephens
Author of *Delay, Don't Deny: Living and Intermittent Fasting Lifestyle*

Welcome from The Smiths

Before we jump into the story, we want to address all of you, our readers. We feel like we're talking to the members of our online IF community, thousands of people we have never met in person who nonetheless have taught, supported and encouraged us through the past 16 months. Writing this book feels similar to addressing the members of our own Facebook IF support group, currently numbering over 2000, all folks with some degree of interest in bettering their lives and their health through intermittent fasting.

Why did we write this book? There are two reasons. First, reading Gin Stephens' book *Delay, Don't Deny: Living an Intermittent Fasting Lifestyle* showed us clearly that one person putting their story out into the world could create ripples of impact. We hoped that two of us telling our interrelated stories could have similar effects.

Second, and maybe more importantly, people asked for this book. We heard over and over that our transformation was amazing, incredible, unbelievable. People looked at our pictures and said, "Wow! You look like two totally different people! How did you do that?" We were asked so many times that we began to ask ourselves. We reflected on where we had come from, our lives before we met, the years of our marriage so far, and the point in the process we had reached. We looked at each other and agreed that yes, this is a story that should be told, especially for those couples who may feel locked in a pattern of using food to deal with life. You too may have found yourself stuck in a rut, gaining weight and feeling powerless to do anything about it.

This book will be more of a memoir than an instructional manual. There is only a smattering of "how to" within these pages. Over these last several years, we have carved our own unique path to get free from food, most notably by using intermittent fasting; it has shown us that each of our bodies and our lifestyles is too unique for there to be a cookie-cutter approach. We will definitely share the things we learned and what worked for us. This book was written in hopes that other people might be encouraged and inspired to make concrete changes to find the freedom and joy we have found.

One more thing to note: this isn't the story of a single dramatic or traumatic event and how we overcame it. It's the story of two people and a thousand tiny tragedies. It's about how we met and married in a flurry of romantic good intentions and then veered so far off course that we were lost in the woods for a decade. We didn't get out of those woods with a clear, definitive map. We wandered and roamed. We backed up and tried another direction until eventually, we realized we were on a trail and it was leading toward a clearing where there was sunlight coming through the trees. We're now basking in the glow of freedom and we are trying to create a guide to pass along.

If there is a single message to glean from this book, it's that if we did it, you can too. We hope you will, and we hope you'll let us know at www.fastingfeastingfreedom.com. Come with us on the journey.

Ryan: The Early Years

For as long as I can remember, my relationship with food was not right. It was never about nutrition or fueling my body. No, my relationship with food can best be described as a love affair. Not a great love affair like Noah and Allie from *The Notebook*. More like Michael Douglas and Glenn Close in *Fatal Attraction*. It started out fun and exciting but took some very dark turns. It was a relationship so dysfunctional and consuming that I expected it to dominate my life forever. I thought I would always be fat and would never be free.

Some people are just meant to be miserable, right? As it turns out, no. Being fat and unhealthy is a symptom of something bigger and more important than what foods you choose to eat or which arbitrary rules you choose to follow. And for me being fat was a symptom of being unhappy rather than the other way around. In the past 15 years, I have lost and regained 120 pounds….twice. Losing weight is pretty easy if you're consistent with a way of eating, but keeping it off is more challenging than I realized it would be. I was stuck on in an on-again-off-again relationship with food until I found a way to eat that not only facilitated weight loss but healed my complicated dynamic with food.

For a long time, I thought that I got fat because I just loved to eat, and truthfully, I did love to eat. Whenever my parents put me and my brother Curt in the car to go shopping, I started doing mental math, calculating the likelihood that we would be out long enough to necessitate a stop at McDonald's for lunch. My parents were not the kind who caved to pressure from the kids, and I knew to ask would make it less likely to happen, so I remained quiet in the back seat, inwardly appealing to the universe to make the car turn in by the golden arches.

While reciting my silent but focused wishes for cheeseburgers, I would listen for tell-tale snippets of adult conversation that might confirm what I was hoping for. It would go something like this. My father would start grumbling about being "faint", and my mother would yield and give her reluctant blessing to stop. The car would turn into the drive-through, and I would be squirming with Christmas morning levels of excitement. I haven't eaten McDonald's food in a long time, but I still remember the anticipation of those lunches, the two cheeseburgers with the little dehydrated onions, the grease, and salt of the fries, plus the overly sweet chemical sensation of diet soda. It was manna from Heaven.

Almost every kid in America loves McDonald's, but for me food was becoming so much more than a fun treat or momentary diversion. I didn't have the words for it at the time, but I was using food to medicate all sorts of feelings. If I was bored, eating would help pass the time. If I wanted a reward, food could do it. Most of all, if I was feeling anxious, eating would put a temporary band-aid on that as well. It's taken me a long time to realize it, but I was a very anxious kid. I grew up with the adults around me describing me as "shy" and other kids constantly pointing out that I was blushing about something. Innocent comments? Probably, but I felt like something was wrong with me, and eating made that feeling go away.

Every year around my July 31st birthday, my mother would bring out the Sears catalog to begin back-to-school shopping. Go through the boys' section and circle the colors you like, she would tell me. I dutifully did so, only to get this inevitable feedback: you have to choose something else. These are not available in….HUSKY PANTS. Two words that strike terror in the heart of every fat kid. Every boy who shopped the husky section knew the label was just a way to avoid speaking aloud the awful truth. You're fat.

Clothes became my enemy and wrestling into a pair of tight pants cinched up with a belt became my daily battle. I saw other kids playing and laughing and being kids, while I was using mental energy worrying whether anyone could hear my legs rubbing together in my Husky corduroys. Seriously, who thought that putting ridges on fat kid clothes was a good idea? Navigating childhood is hard enough without adding the fear of spontaneous combustion to the mix. I got through each day by sucking in my gut until I could get home and have a snack.

8

We used to visit my Grampie and Grammie Smith every other weekend. I loved my grandparents, but it was mind-numbingly boring for a kid. I would play with the small assortment of toys that my grandmother kept in a bucket in the bedroom while scheming new and inventive ways to pass by the candy dish to pilfer more mints. The pink ones were my favorite, but the white and green ones could push back a nasty feeling in a pinch.

My real attention was on the time. I knew that if the clock reached a certain point, my grandmother would disappear into the kitchen to cook a meal. She never asked if we would like to stay for dinner; it was an unspoken agreement. If you stick around long enough, you get fed.

I loved those meals at Grammie's house. The food was different and somehow better. She made traditional big meals at noon-time and light suppers in the evening. I thought this was the cleverest innovation known to man. What could be better than a huge spread with meat and potatoes, gravy and pickles and bread and butter, all in the middle of the day when there would still be time to wait a few hours then eat again? Genius.

One particular time when I was around 12 years old, we were done eating dinner and had moved onto dessert. I don't remember what the actual treat was, but I'm sure it involved Cool Whip, and I'm sure I loved it. As I was riding the high, my grandfather abruptly and loudly announced, "Ryan, you're getting fat!" Ouch. Thanks, Grampie. It was true, but still stung to hear it out loud.

Everyone laughed awkwardly and tried to gloss it over, but it burned. I already knew that being "chubby" was not a small thing, no pun intended, but somehow, I thought that people didn't really notice. Sure, my belt was threatening to cut me in half like a magician's assistant, but it was my own personal cross to bear. It felt like my grandfather, in one moment of ornery, misguided honesty, had outed me to the world as FAT. I wanted to crawl into a hole and bury myself with peanut butter cups.

Being a fat kid is rough but being a fat teenager is worse. By the time I reached high school, I started to figure out that the whole "you just have big bones" line was a bigger crock than" If you're really good, Santa will bring it". I was watching my classmates move into the world of dating and parties, and I wanted my life to become the 80's style teen movie I thought their lives were. I was more Chunk from *The Goonies* than Ferris Bueller, so I decided to do something about it.

My only source of weight loss information was my mother, and unfortunately, the diet and fitness industry had been lying to her for years. It was like asking Mr. Magoo for driving lessons. Anyone remember the little booklets from the checkout line that listed the calorie counts for all the foods? Check. How about the torture contraption of ropes and pulleys hooked to a doorknob that forced your arms and legs into the air without the pesky need for muscular contractions? My mom had one. Mint condition. Stationary bike? Mini trampoline? Purple rubber 5-pound dumbbells? She had those, too. It was the 80's, so I'm sure there was a Thigh Master in the house somewhere.

Somehow, I reached the conclusion that 1800 calories per day and 45 minutes of flailing around the basement, jumping from one piece of equipment to the next, was the magic sweet spot for fitness. I was one sparkly leotard away from completely transforming into Suzanne Somers. That summer was consumed with counting and recording. How many calories in a grape? Better take one off the plate, or I will go over the limit. Got off the bike on minute 43? Better luck tomorrow. It was crazy-making, but in terms of losing weight, it worked.

I lost 30 pounds that summer, and while I did like the fact that people noticed, I treated the whole experience like a drunken bender in Vegas. I was embarrassed about how I took the weight off and would make veiled references to "eating better" and "working out". I wanted to be perceived as the popular jock in the movie, not the cool kid's middle-aged mom, imitating Jane Fonda.

Within a few months, it didn't matter anyway because what I was doing was so restrictive, so driven by rules and so ill-informed about how the body actually works, that it was destined to fail. When school started up in the fall, I went back to old habits and abandoned all my new ones. I regained all the weight, and then some, before the glow of the compliments even wore off. I welcomed back my old friend procrastination with open arms, figuring that high school was lost to me, even though I had two years left to go. I settled into my comfortable role of the shy, fat kid, while entertaining fantasies of how college would be different. It was the beginning of a long pattern of planning action but never taking any.

My mother set up a tropical fish aquarium in the living room as something we could "do" together as a family. It was fun watching all the different kinds of fish swimming around in there, many with distinct behaviors and personalities. The angelfish were colorful and confident, rushing to the side to stare back at observers. The gourami fish were cocky and aggressive, biting the others on the backside whenever they drifted by. Then there were the sucker fish, whose main mission in life was to quietly clean algae off the side of the tank. They were not much to look at, didn't display any personality, and generally went unnoticed by the other fish. For many years, I saw myself in those fish.

I hoped that I would somehow be a new person in college, but the anxiety and social awkwardness I felt growing up was actually worse, when friends were no longer "built into" the experience. I made the decision to live at home and commute to school to save money, and while it was a sound financial choice, it made it easy to isolate myself from other people and new experiences.

I was on a bustling college campus every day, surrounded by people, but would routinely go days with no meaningful social interaction. I came out my hiding places long enough to attend class then dart into full retreat before anyone noticed me. I was probably around 200 pounds, but the weight on me was far more than physical. It felt to me like I was destined to be that sucker fish forever, lonely and alone, picking away at the scraps of life.

Looking back now, I realize that my biggest problem was a complete lack of action. I was waiting for something to happen, but I expected it to happen magically, without effort on my part. The fact that it wasn't easy felt like a kick-me-when-I'm-down situation. I remained a silent observer of the lives of others, constantly judging, comparing, and wishing for something to somehow fix me.

There was this guy in one of my first-year lecture classes. I don't remember which class, but I can still see him in my mind's eye so clearly. He was a tall, muscular football player type. I called him Chip because he seemed like the living embodiment of the popular jock in every high school movie ever made, Johnny from *The Karate Kid* without the anger management issues. I have no idea who he really was or what his life was truly like. I only saw the surface trappings, and I was insanely jealous. To me, his life was one long series of high fives and hot dates.

Chip became a very important person in my life, even though we never exchanged a word, and as far as I know, he never even looked in my direction. I didn't like being me, and I worked hard to convince myself that if I lost the weight, I could be him. A silly and dysfunctional coping mechanism for sure, but recasting Chip in the role of my life gave me a misguided sense of hope that things could be better. It would be many years and many pints of ice cream before I figured out that losing weight wouldn't change my life into a movie plot, but at the time, it allowed to continue putting one foot in front of the other. I don't know where Chip is now, but I owe him a debt of gratitude.

My obsessive food behavior escalated rapidly. People use the word "addiction" freely and lightly, so I will leave it to scientists and doctors to debate the mechanics of food and sugar addiction. I do know that food was WAY more important to me than it should have been. I was eating instead of engaging with other people. I lied and covered up my food behavior. I ate to avoid feeling things I didn't want to feel. I felt a deep and consuming shame about all of it. Draw your own conclusions about whether food addiction is real, but my behavior was self-destructive, no matter what you call it.

I worked at a small family-owned grocery store called Nutter's Market for most of my high school and college years. Much like an alcoholic hanging out in a bar, I worked at the store in part because it gave me constant access to snacks. I stayed in the back of the walk-in coolers most of the time, putting soda on the shelves, and drinking a fair amount of it myself. Nothing cultivates a Mountain Dew habit like towering cases of the stuff and a dark cool place to enjoy it. I could peer out to see and hear customers as they came in to buy supplies for whatever fun excursion I imagined they were having, and when the coast was clear, I could come out to grab something to eat. I hope the statute of limitations on grand theft whoopie pie has expired because the LaBree's chocolate-vanilla three-pack saw me through a lot of dark days.

Don't get me wrong, I was a model employee in most ways. I cared very much about what people thought of me, so I worked hard to do a good job. But I worked just as hard to conceal how unhappy I was and how much food played a role in it. I probably wasn't fooling anyone. After all, I was displaying my sadness all over my body, but it was a game I would continue to play for several more years.

After I graduated from college and started my teaching career, my twisted love affair with food escalated. I was living alone, and making my own money, and that translated to a lot of excessive eating. By this point, I wasn't really eating meals anymore. I didn't eat at all during the school day because I was far too self-conscious to eat in front of other people. Instead, I would internalize the stresses of the day and think about what I would eat later. I stopped at the grocery store every night for supplies for my daily binge. There was an air of desperation around it. White knuckling it through the day, worrying that I wouldn't have "enough" food to make it until bedtime, eating until I was stuffed and sick but saving just a little bit for the next morning, then repeating it the next day.

When I first told Kim about one of these binges, she was amazed at the sheer volume of food that I was consuming. My typical strategy was to buy a mini meal, something like Hot Pockets and a bag of candy, to tide me over while the main event was

13

cooking. Sometimes I bought a family pack of chicken or pork chops, two boxes of cheddar flavored rice, and a pint of Ben & Jerry's. While I was putting all this food into my cart, I would mentally rehearse the story I would tell if I ran into someone I knew. The family pack of meat? Oh, my parents are coming for a visit. The mega-bag of peanut butter cups? Just stocking up for Halloween. All of my eating was done at home in secret. Surprisingly I never got takeout pizza or fast food drive-thru. Why not? Too much risk that one of my students would be working the window and see evidence that Mr. Smith eats. As if the 250 pounds I was carrying around was not proof enough. It was insanity.

Teaching was my rock during this time in my life. My first position was in a small town in rural Maine. The students were distrustful of me at first, but I won them over. I felt like my work with kids was the only thing giving my life value. I was good at it, and I cultivated connections with colleagues and students that sustained me through a lot of days when I didn't have much else. As the sole English teacher in the school, I was expected to put on school plays for the community and publish a student newspaper. Both of these things were miles away from my comfort zone, but it provided an anchor in an otherwise adrift existence.

On the other hand, it was enormously stressful to be in front of the classroom. I was physically uncomfortable, perpetually self-conscious and expending a ton of mental energy on hiding the way I was living and eating outside of school. High school kids are funny and clever, but they can also be thoughtless and sometimes downright mean. One day I was moving along a crowded row of desks when the intercom system beeped. Right on cue, a student said, "Look out, he's backing up". Total silence as a whole class of kids waits on my reaction. I ignored it, but I will never forget it. It was eerily reminiscent of my grandfather calling me fat almost 15 years earlier, a confirmation that despite all my efforts to pretend otherwise, people could see how heavy I was. I wasn't fooling anyone.

By age 29, I weighed 278 pounds, and I had given up on losing weight. I read a lot of diet books and made a lot of plans, but

I never lasted more than a day on any of them. Then I received a call from my doctor's office that changed everything. The medical assistant's voice was light and friendly, which somehow made the news even more alarming. "Your fasting blood sugar is 310. Please make an appointment to come in to discuss meds."

I was devastated because it was a confirmation of what I already knew. I wasn't a kid anymore. I wasn't going to "grow out of it". I realized that my weight wasn't just about how I looked or what kind of clothes I could fit into. It was actually threatening my life. My mind was flooded with a variety of gory images. My feet falling off. My internal organs shutting down. My impending death. Probably an overreaction, but I'm grateful that it got my attention. One of my darkest fears was that I could die in my apartment and nobody would find me for days. The diabetes diagnosis made that irrational fear more real and motivated me to make some changes.

I had been interested in vegetarianism for years, so when my doctor asked what I was willing to do to get healthy, I vowed to stop reading about it and actually become it. Overnight I changed my diet from mountains of fatty meat and processed carbs to whole grains, beans and loads of veggies. I also threw myself into a new exercise program, doing workout videos at least five times a week.

Since I was changing up my identity from carnivore to herbivore anyway, I also wholeheartedly embraced the persona of "good diabetic". I religiously tested my blood sugar, took my meds without fail and meticulously tracked my carb intake. I discovered that diabetes is a HUGE industry and stocked up on the latest products, like fun flavored glucose tablets and multi-colored lancets for pricking my finger. I was probably a tad obsessed, but in terms of my weight and overall health, it was working for me.

Back in high school, I had taken tenth-grade Biology with a teacher who was renowned for being tough. Her exam on the human digestive system consisted of one question. Describe the complete metabolic process of digesting a hamburger from the first bite to its exit from the body. It was known to be a grueling test that nobody could defeat. I got a 99 on that test. I lost one point for failing to mention the word "feces" in the last sentence of the last paragraph of the four pages of narrative that otherwise captured every enzyme, every chemical composition, every internal organ. You might say that I aced most of the test, but I didn't deal with my shit.

That was also the case for my life during that first major weight loss. Sure, I lost 120 pounds, my blood sugar readings were soon better than normal, and I got off the diabetes meds easily. I was earning an A from my doctors and other people around me who labeled me an inspiration, but I was approaching the whole thing the wrong way. I was still using food to manage my time and my emotions, I was just eating healthier food. I was exercising regularly, but I hated every minute of it. I still felt deeply embarrassed about how fat I had become even when it wasn't literally true anymore. It didn't occur to me at the time that my loneliness, anxiety, and shame were the real problems, and I was putting a more effective, but ultimately, a temporary band-aid on my situation.

On the surface I was trying to play it cool and play the part of a thin man. I started to make other positive changes in my life. I enrolled in graduate school to get a Master's degree in counselor education. It was that decision that proved to be the most important one of all because it led me to meet my wife Kimberly. When I met Kim, I was thin, and I thought my issues with weight were behind me. I had convinced myself that I had found the mythical weight loss answer and my days of being a prisoner of food were behind. In reality, it was the beginning of a journey we were now taking together.

Kim: The Early Years

Picture a little girl standing on the sidelines while other children gleefully participate in a sack race on field day. She is smaller than the others by a bit, with big blue eyes and a solemn expression. She is watching intently and inside, she is praying that she can avoid being noticed and forced into line to take the next turn.

That little girl is me, and looking back at my childhood self, a pervasive sense of uneasiness dominates my memories. Neither food nor weight were particularly prominent themes, but anxiety was. In today's environment, my emotional and behavioral presentation likely would have led to a diagnosis of some kind. I was considered bright, an early reader who could spell "neighborhood" before Kindergarten. However, I was frequently off-task, daydreaming, observing and overthinking when my peers were simply playing and being kids.

Within my family, I was thought of as articulate, great at telling funny stories, but less active and adventurous than my cousins who liked to climb rocks and swim way out into deep waters. I was always scared that something bad would happen to them or to me. I remember simply worrying - a lot. I worried whether the house would burn down or if I might get kidnapped. The Adam Walsh story terrified me. Worst case scenarios ran through my mind as far back as I can remember.

I even worried about small things like getting a splinter. After listening to my cousin scream while having one extracted on the other side of a closed door, I got a splinter of my own and hid it from my parents. I was terrified of the pain of having it pulled out with tweezers after how my cousin had reacted. I would wait until everyone went to bed and then creep to the bathroom, where I would set up a makeshift medical clinic, soaking my foot in a basin of hot water and hydrogen peroxide and praying for the sliver to come out on its own. I had heard a bit of wood could work its way into my bloodstream and eventually pierce my heart. I can't remember if or how the splinter got out of my sore foot, but I remember those bleary-eyed, exhausted nights, agonizing on the cold linoleum while everyone slept. I can chuckle over it now, but I also feel sad for that scared little girl.

Of course, food was part of my life, and I have happy memories that involve special meals, but there's only a little to say about my childhood relationship with food. I don't remember food being a particular source of coping or comfort during those years. I was a fairly picky eater, and it was the late 70's to mid-80s, an era where people were beginning to favor the convenience of packaged foods. That time was dominated by Hamburger Helper, Spaghetti-Os, canned Vienna sausages, Kool-Aid, and Tang made from (literally) colored sugar. My grandmother cooked traditional homemade meals, but she would also make pizza with Spam on top for our birthdays. This memory elicits expression of disgust from those I share it with, but we loved it.

I had certain special favorites my mother would make for me at home, like cream cheese and olive sandwiches with the crusts cut off. I think that may be why I love cream cheese with green olives to this day. The same is true for oatmeal, which I still love. My dad would stop for cigarettes and buy me a chocolate milk, something that remained a comfort food into adulthood. When I think of childhood and food in the same sentence, mostly processed treats come to mind.

My happy memories of my grandparents' house were about food but also about the oasis of tranquility that their home represented for me. Otherwise anxious and uneasy, I remember feeling soothed by how warm and calm it was in their home. My father's parents were always in their kitchen humming and working, preparing meals in the tiny space like a little choreographed dance. My grandmother actually lived to be 95, passing away just before my 40th birthday, and walking into her home made me feel tranquil right up until the last weeks of her life.

During years when I struggled to feel good about myself, my grandmother was always there to make me feel like the star of the show. She meant more to me than I realized, and in her final years, as she implored me to simply enjoy my life, I became motivated to do just that. The positive life changes I made in her honor led directly to us writing this book, which is why the book is dedicated to her. Three simple words, enjoy your life, have become my mantra.

My parents spent several tumultuous years together, then divorced when I was in middle school. Divorce is a large enough theme in my story that I consider it my culture, the way some people identify with their ethnic ancestry or their religion. At that point, Mum returned to work after a stint running a daycare to be home with my younger sister, Mary. It was a very stressful time for her, being the sole custodial parent to two teenagers and a little kid without a lot of help. Dad had a busy job and we didn't spend much time with him after he moved out. He was always available to us by phone and he supported us financially, but there was not a schedule of regular visits. Like so many things I would change, I wish I had spent more time with Dad during those years, but it was a strained situation for us all.

While Mary attended childcare after school and Mum worked, my brother Jeff and I ate a lot of cold cereal and to an extent, "fended for ourselves." There were always foods around that we could heat up in the microwave easily. We frequently ate in front of the TV; we watched every rerun of the Brady Bunch at least three times. We bickered a great deal, but Jeff was a constant companion during the latchkey days.

I fondly remember eating favorite sweets, like Mum's butterscotch Scotch-a-roos and Gram's M&M cookies, and occasionally, I overdid it with sugar. Otherwise, I have only a few early memories of dysfunctional behavior around food. There was a restaurant with a famous all-you-can-eat buffet in our town and occasionally, I was invited to eat there with a friend's family. I recall overeating to the point of discomfort and having my first feelings of regret about food choices and amounts. My friend and I unbuttoned our pants in bloated misery on the ride home, something I'd never done before, but unfortunately an action I would end up taking many times in the future.

I was always a good student, bright but distracted, performing well on report cards. There was only one class I truly dreaded: physical education. During middle school, my aversion bordered on a mild phobia. Just like hopping in a burlap sack on field day, weekly PE class felt like a humiliating spectacle. I felt clumsy and awkward enough that I never voluntarily participated in sports, even individual ones. It is tough to sort out how much of this was social anxiety, not liking to be looked at, and how much was about my distinct lack of "kinesthetic intelligence." While this wasn't about being overweight, it was absolutely about lack of confidence in myself and a feeling of disconnection from my body that would play a role in future struggles.

There is a strong tie between shame and perfectionism, and I now realize that the fears were rooted in worry that my ineptitude at sports was evidence of my unworthiness. I recently read that there is a strong correlation between feelings about Phys Ed classes and lifetime attitudes toward exercise. This resonated with me because I was in my 40's before I learned to truly enjoy moving my body for its own sake.

Size-wise, I was always one of the smallest students in my class, not reaching my peak adult height of 5'3" until age 14. That was the same age that my weight finally reached 100 pounds and I got my first period; I was the last among my friends for that milestone. During 8th grade year, I received a fair amount of positive attention about the way my body was developing, and it being awkward and thrilling at the same time.

After puberty, I gained weight steadily, starting high school in the ballpark of 125-130 pounds. This was a reasonable weight for my build, so I can't say why I decided it was too much, but I did. My mother was not a chronic or restrictive dieter, which is where many young women say the message came from. Likewise, my friends weren't obsessed with appearance or thinness, but somehow the message from society got in my head that slimmer was better.

I chose to follow the Weight Watchers old school plan, using castoff materials from one of my mother's friends. You could have like one pat of butter for the entire day and you'd filled your fat exchange. Armed with a pencil and checkboxes for the different categories, I managed to get 20 pounds back off by obsessively restricting and tracking what I ate. Dieting isn't easy for anyone, but it is a major drag when you are a picky eater who doesn't like salad or vegetables much. I shudder at the memory of the low fat, low-calorie way I ate over those months. I recall a lot of dry tuna fish, canned green beans eaten with no salt or butter, and a fair amount of misery.

I also remember wearing a bikini that summer and feeling attractive in it. I was 16 years old and enjoying a short-lived stint of feeling confident about my body. Within a year of that time, I started dating a boy named Matt, who is now my former husband. We spent our time hanging out with friends, eating pizza and fast food, all the strict Weight Watchers protocols pushed aside. I was not really worrying about my weight, but not feeling great about myself, either. Though I hate now to admit it, I think there was a bit of 'I found a boyfriend, so I don't have to worry about that stuff in the same way' going on, which says a lot about where my life went next.

My high school years were the best and worst for me. I don't know if it is common to have such mixed feelings looking back, but I do. I was a straight-A student and thrived under the positive attention of teachers. I waited eagerly for the honor roll every quarter. That same perfectionism that said "you are worthy if you are producing results" was soothed by good grades on tests and glowing comments on papers. The classroom wasn't the only place I flourished; I was involved in many clubs and served as editor of my high school yearbook. I admired my teachers and thought very seriously about studying to become one.

Though my relationship with Matt was fraught with silly, immature spats, it was pretty typical for a teenage dating situation and similar to the dynamics of the other couples around us. We had our share of good times, watching tons of movies, countless episodes of Saturday Night Live, and attending each other's proms. We were pretty straight-laced kids who didn't party, drink or do drugs, but I was unhealthily focused on our relationship to avoid stress at home.

In retrospect, issues at home drove me to make major life choices that changed my whole trajectory.

My mother remarried during my junior year of high school, which was a tough transition for all of us. My brother Jeff, though very intelligent, struggled in school and chose to go live with friends at age 16. Mary was nine at the time; because my stepfather was not used to having a young child underfoot, there was frequent tension in the household. I dealt with all of this by rarely being home, working my part-time job and being with Matt or other friends.

Though I won a full academic scholarship to our state university, my driving motivation was not related to my education or my future career. When I look back on the weeks leading up to my high school graduation, I recall feeling in a hurry to be an adult and looking down my nose at peers who seemed to care so much about graduation itself. I just wanted to "start my life", all of which led me to marry Matt by age 20 and to become a mother by age 22.

During college and through my 20s, my weight yo-yoed between 140-160 lbs. I was fortunate to have two healthy pregnancies, though I definitely could have eaten more wholesome food and stayed more active than I did. My first baby, Adam, was born in 1996 by C-section after a long, grueling labor. Being induced for high blood pressure created, as they say, a "cascade of interventions" - being bed-bound with close monitoring, the need for extra pain medication - but I think my sense of weakness and disconnection from my body played a role, too. I felt like a failure for not giving birth in what I considered the natural way, and I was mildly depressed for the first several months after his birth.

With my second pregnancy, overwhelmed with a struggling marriage and the prospect of two babies by age 25, I asked early on about a permanent sterilization. The plan was for scheduled C-section and a tubal ligation, all to be calmly performed on a Monday morning. Instead, my water broke the Saturday night beforehand and I found myself being whisked off to surgery nearing midnight on May Day 1999. Two important milestones happened inside that operating room: my Emma Lorraine was born, and my Fallopian tubes were clamped and cut as I had asked.

Young motherhood was difficult for me. My babies were healthy, but neither was a good sleeper. I say I didn't have a solid night of uninterrupted sleep for five straight years. The fatigue exacerbated my baseline anxiety. If you are someone who worried about splinters, how stressful is being responsible for two small children with all that can possibly go wrong? I had not had enough time and space to work through my own issues nor finish my identity development before I became a mother. Yet, I loved my babies fiercely. I put intense pressure on myself to be a good mom and give them both everything they needed.

Both kids were breastfed, but once they were weaned, they basically ate the same kinds of foods I ate. There were no considerations about whether baby food was organic or contained GMOs; it wasn't even something I thought about. I didn't worry much about my own nutrition or theirs, as long as we all ate something every day. It was a bit of a survival mode at that time. We had happy days, but I still look back and wish I'd enjoyed the little moments more.

When I could not find a job using my English degree, my mother paid for me to take a medical transcription training course through a local trade school. The hope at the time I signed up was that I could work while at home while caring for the children. It was one of many efforts she made to help me get my life on track during young adulthood, and though it didn't pan into a career at that point, it would later turn out to be a fortuitous thing for me.

Between the financial pressures and the stress of two young children, Matt and I fought a lot -not the bickering from my days with my brother, not the silly spats of high school, but genuine, serious conflicts. I felt profoundly unhappy during those years. It felt like I was a hamster in a wheel, frantically trying to be happy, seeing it like some mythical destination on the horizon that I ran and ran but could not get any closer to reaching. I'm certain poor Matt had no idea what to do with me. He was younger when we got married than our son Adam is now. I look at Adam and while I'm so proud of the young man he has become, I do not see him as mature enough to enter into something as serious as marriage.

I'm sure I felt like I was fat during those years, and I probably complained about my weight, but not enough to change my eating behavior in any meaningful way. I had very little useful information about nutrition to apply to my eating plan. Brief crash diets happened here and there, though my specific motivation is hard to pinpoint, much like my initial foray into Weight Watchers in high school. I would end up losing 10 pounds and regaining 15. There was a brief membership to a women's gym a la Curves with my former mother-in-law; as I used the cardio equipment, I felt sweaty and miserable, despising every minute. I had a touch of exercised-induced asthma that increased my discomfort with cardio exercise.

Overall, though, general unhappiness dominated my thoughts in my 20s far more than weight or body image issues. I followed my preferences from childhood, eating junk and convenience foods far beyond my college days. I taught myself to cook a few meals from scratch, but I mostly stuck with the familiar, making omelets or tacos and fixing oh-so-many packages of Kraft Macaroni and Cheese. Our budget was tight, so these were the foods we could afford. I rarely bought fresh produce or quality cuts of meat. Financial constraints ingrained my quick, cheap eating habits even deeper.

After seven years of struggling through a young marriage for which neither of us was ready, Matt and I separated in 2001. Adam was then 5 and Emma was 2. Following my divorce, I found myself in a world of practical and emotional chaos. "Fending for myself" took on a whole new meaning. We had struggled financially trying to live on Matt's income and at the time we split, I did not have a job outside the home. The kids and I moved frequently, first staying with a friend, then in a small apartment. Survival mode took on a new meaning, too. I barely had a plan beyond the day we were living in.

These were the most defining years of my entire life. Being a young mother on my own with two little kids was terrifying. But

24

man, oh man, the drive I felt to figure things out for them pushed me through those tough days. As I woke each morning, a sick dread flooded in as I remembered my reality. I would stare up at the ceiling, wondering how to get through the day, let alone the next 15 years. How had I gone from being a promising honor student to a flat-broke divorcee in less than a decade? The sadness and hopelessness were so overwhelming that I would pull the covers over my head, trying to go back to sleep and shut it all out. Instead, there would be a tugging on those blankets and I would peer out to two little faces. They were depending on me to get up and moving, so I put one foot in front of the other. I genuinely believe that having my kids to love and care for saved my life during my darkest days.

Looking back on those years feels like ancient history now. I almost look at that young woman hustling to survive like a stranger, but she was me and I am her. Because I didn't have any better ideas (and because school had always been my happy place), I enrolled in graduate school at my alma mater, the University of Maine. As a single mom with no income, student loan money came rolling in right away. In an ironic way, grad school turned an awful time in my life into an exciting one. After attending college with all my focus on becoming a wife and mom, grad school was giving me a chance to get involved in campus culture.

I know I was eating liberally during this time, college-type food like nachos and pizza. I also started to drink lots of wine, something I had never done until after my divorce. My weight went all the way up into the mid-180s, a weight I had only seen in late pregnancy, and I was not happy about it. I vowed to myself: I CANNOT let my weight get this close to 200 pounds ever again (little did I know there would be a point in the future when I'd be trying desperately to get BACK DOWN to 200).

I mustered up that Monday-of-a-new-diet motivation and bought a paperback copy of *The Carbohydrate Addict's Diet* by Dr. Richard and Rachel Heller. I read the book and started following their plan in an attempt to get sugar and starch cravings under control. I ate those salads I'd always avoided; I read labels. In an attempt to cut carb counts and for that long-sought convenience, I bought numerous Atkins bars each week. I started a ritual of doing Mari Winsor Pilates daily.

By the beginning of the spring semester in 2003, I was making new friends and doing things socially when the kids went with their dad. I had lost about 25 pounds for the umpteenth time and I was feeling pretty good about myself for the first time in what seemed like forever. The divorce and the initial adjustments were behind me and I felt ready to move forward. I hoped I would meet a man who wanted to start a new life with me and my growing kids.

Meeting and Marriage

Kim and I met in graduate school, specifically a career counseling course, that began in January of 2003. Technically we didn't meet until April of that year, but we were in the class at the same time, and as it turns out, very aware of the other's presence. I remember clearly the first moment I saw her and the first things she said when she introduced herself to the class. She was a newly-divorced single mother trying to make a better life for herself and her two children. I was immediately attracted to her. She was cute and smart, and she radiated enthusiasm for the topic, a passion of hers to this day. Unfortunately, I was clueless that she might feel the same about me. After years of being significantly overweight, I had become accustomed to going unnoticed, and it never occurred to me that my interest could be mutual.

Unbeknownst to me, Kim was talking about me to her friends, and they were encouraging her to make a move. She tells me that at first, she was hindered by her insecurities. What if this guy is already in a relationship? What if he's gay? What if he's just not interested? I'm very grateful that she decided to ignore those voices because it changed the trajectory of our entire lives.

Kim sent me an email inviting me to have coffee after class. Her tone was breezy and friendly, and I was instantly thrilled and nervous. I didn't consider declining for an instant, but I did over-analyze my response. It was so important to me to nail that email, to make just the right impression. From the very beginning of our relationship, I somehow knew that what Kim thought of me would be the most important opinion in my life.

I waited two days to reply, so as not to appear over-eager or desperate. I wrote and revised that email with meticulous detail before I sent it, going for the perfect balance of warmth and confidence. At the time, I didn't drink coffee, but I accepted the offer and suggested that we meet up after class the following week. We settled on the Oakes Room cafe in the Raymond H. Fogler Library just across the quad from our classroom.

There are defining moments in life that take root in the memory so deeply that they play and replay like a movie scene. For me, one of those moments arrived as I approached the Union for class on the day we were planning to go for coffee. As I reached for the door to enter the building, Kim came out on her way back to her car to retrieve something.

I had rehearsed in my head the moment we would see each other in class, so this deviation from the plan could have really thrown me off. Instead, I said something like, "Oh, I'll walk along with you", and we started chatting as we walked. Later Kim told me that this struck her as supremely confident, as though I must have had first dates all the time. Definitely not, but there was something about her that brought out something new in me. I felt like I knew her before I knew her.

That first conversation that continued in the cafe after class was magical to me. She told me that she felt everything happens for a reason. I told her that I wasn't sure about that, but I thought life was about finding meaning in the things that do happen to us. She told me about her beloved grandmother and her children and her ambition to work with college students. I talked to her about teaching and books and a desire to go skydiving. It was easy and fun, deep and meaningful, and she was so cute. She looked at me with an expression that blew me away, and I think I knew immediately that I wanted to do whatever I had to do to keep earning that look on her face.

We were still looking over the menu on our first official date when Kim told me that she had her tubes tied after she had her second child. She wanted to be clear that she couldn't have more children in case that was a deal breaker for me. I had always dreamed of having a wife and children, but I was never particularly invested in passing along my genetics. I knew in an instant that I wanted her, and I wanted a family, but I didn't care about making a baby of my own.

Of course, I was nervous about meeting her children, and she wanted to be sure of where our relationship was going before

28

bringing me into their lives, but Adam and Emma were a central part of our love story from that moment on. Being a mother was the most important thing in Kim's life, and her devotion to her children was a big reason I was so drawn to her. I realized that as I was falling in love with her, I was also falling in love with two little people I had never even met.

The first time Kim introduced me to the children, it was an instant connection. Adam was seven years old, and Emma had just turned four. They were as warm and open to me as their mother, and it was clear that they were happy and accepting individuals because of her. We took them to walk the trail at a local park. Adam slipped his hand into mine without hesitation, and Emma climbed into my arms like a little monkey on a tree.

Our first summer together was a whirlwind of spending time alone together when the kids were with their father and spending time as a new little family when the kids were with Kim. We'd spend entire days going to the ocean or watching movies or just hanging out talking about our lives and dreams, then fill the evenings making dinner for the children, taking them out for ice cream or watching cartoons together. It was the best of both worlds, and I loved it.

Food and weight also became a central theme in our relationship early on. I was months into maintenance after losing 120 pounds with a mostly vegetarian diet. Kim had taken off 25 pounds with the Carbohydrate Addict's Diet. Both of us felt like we had solved our weight problems, but we were naive about how those two different ways of eating and our individual issues around food and weight would mesh in the new life we were creating together. Kim knew me as a health-focused person, so she tried to eat the way I did, although she didn't really like the foods I was eating. She tells me she didn't want me to know about her long-term junk food habit.

The first meal I made for her was salmon and a huge salad of dark, leafy greens. I had never cooked salmon before, but I thought it would impress her, so I researched how to do it. She was impressed by my ability to cook a meal for her, but it was years before she confessed that she didn't like the taste of the fish or the greens in the salad. She recollects chewing and chewing, trying to get through the big bowl of roughage.

I also struggled with how to maintain my weight loss with so many disruptions to my carefully-structured diet. I started neglecting the carb counting that kept my blood sugar under control. I was eating extra bites of this or that from the kids' plates. At the time, I was happy and thus, I felt overconfident that I could get away with cheating more often.

The first time Kim and I got on a scale in front of each other should have been a red flag that our weight issues were not resolved. At that point, I weighed about 165 pounds. She weighed a few pounds less than me. It was very important for her to weigh less than I did, no matter what the number actually was. I think that was the beginning of a dynamic that would escalate over the next several years. If we gained weight, we would do it together. As long as I was the heavier one, then it was somehow ok. I don't think either of us recognized what a truly slippery slope we were on.

Despite the early warnings that food and weight were a big challenge for us, we were mostly oblivious to it. We were happy and caught up in the romantic aspects of our story together. It looked like a whirlwind to those observing us, and it felt like one in the best possible ways. As the end of the summer of 2003 approached, we realized that we didn't want to begin a new school year with me living and teaching in a town 35 minutes away.

I asked Kim to marry me by playing her a song called "She's the One" by Robbie Williams. I discovered the song a couple of years before and wanted to find the right person to share it with. I marveled at the idea that she was out there the whole time until the stars aligned to bring us together. When I was singing along to that song, missing someone I hadn't even met yet, it was her. I knew that Kim was the one for me, and I didn't want to waste any more time. I asked, she said yes, then we went together to pick out a ring and tell the world.

We decided to move in together right away. We began planning a wedding for the one-year anniversary of our first coffee date at the Oakes Room, but on a romantic impulse, we decided to get married over the holidays in that same calendar year in which we'd met. It just felt that meant to be. Kim's grandmother referred to me as her "intended" and boasted to people that her granddaughter was "marrying a schoolteacher." We still smile at the charming simplicity of that moment. It seemed like everything about our relationship was touched by joy. We got married on December 6, 2003, in a small ceremony in our home, surrounded by the children, our parents, and our closest family.

In retrospect, Kim and I were moving very fast. We met in April, got engaged in August and got married in December...of the same year! If any of our friends or family thought we were nuts, they didn't tell us. Not that it would have mattered to us anyway. We were happy to be together and blissfully unaware of the challenges that awaited us.

Gaining Together

In the early phase of our marriage, our commitment to eating well and being healthy took a backseat to the new happiness we were sharing and the finagling of new routines as a family. It just didn't seem as important to monitor food intake or carb counts or workouts in the face of getting kids to school, dinner and bath rituals, and bedtime stories.

I tried to continue my mostly vegetarian lifestyle, but Kim was not a vegetarian, and the kids even less so. Kim had lost weight by eating low carb for breakfast and lunch, then eating whatever she wanted for her evening meal. While these plans had been successful for us individually, our two styles of eating didn't mesh well. The kids' eating preferences had not changed even as Kim had worked to lose weight, so there was plenty of Mac & cheese and chicken nuggets on our table.

It wasn't long before I announced that I was ready to eat red meat again, leading to a family trip to Wendy's for hamburgers. I started drinking soda again. We veered further and further off our plans. At first, our weight remained stable despite our indulgences, and when the initial regain began, it was slow and easy to ignore, but it wouldn't stay that way.

Kim remembers wanting to hide her food-related indiscretions from me. She told me a story of one day when she was dipping into some cookie dough in the fridge. When she heard my car pull into the driveway, she scooped out a handful with her bare hand, snapped the lid back on, then ran upstairs so she could eat it before I entered the house. She was embarrassed at the idea of me catching her in the act. Who wants to find his new bride elbow deep in a bucket of cookie dough? We may have thought we were hiding from each other, but over time, these bad habits became the norm, and the weight began to pile on rapidly.

Our family reality during the early years was a mix of two worlds. The kids divided their time between our house during the week and their dad's house on the weekend. This was a great arrangement in a lot of ways. We felt more comfortable having the kids with us during the school week, so we could be hands-on for school drop-offs and monitoring meals and homework, but we also cherished our kid-free time. We had the chance to be newlyweds with time and space to focus on each other.

Unfortunately, the custody arrangement was mostly informal and unpredictable, so the children were often the focus of our attention even when they were not with us. We were responsible for most of the kids' transportation and their schedules varied from week to week, so we often felt "on call", like we were waiting around for pick-up time, instead of spending meaningful time together. We quickly fell into patterns of using food as entertainment while we were waiting for the kids to come home.

Our weekend indulgences soon became planned binges. We would drop the kids off at their father's house then head to a grocery store for provisions. This would often take the form of several meals' worth of food to eat in one night. We frequently ordered the Applebee's 2 for $20 deal, usually heavy fried food and fatty dressings, or similar food from a chain place. Sometimes we bought more than one dessert to eat the same evening, staggered out over several hours. We ate a lot and always had a lot more on reserve just in case.

One of our favorite rituals was the Sunday morning food run. We would get up and drive through McDonald's for Egg McMuffins, then hit Dunkin Donuts for donuts and iced coffees. Perhaps we didn't recognize it for what it was at the time, but we were quickly descending into a serious problem with sugar. Like any addiction, there were elements of denial, enabling, and codependency. We could talk ourselves, or each other, into any number of poor food choices. Sometimes we would order not one or two donuts, but a full dozen, telling ourselves it was cheaper per donut that way. We conveniently ignored the true cost of eating all that sugar and lard.

It became clear that we were using food to avoid dealing with the harsher realities of our life together. We loved each other, but we were unprepared for how hard it would be to merge our lives. We got together so quickly that we were caught up in the romantic notion of our story and didn't talk about a lot of the practical things that would cause issues for us. Food was one of them, but we also disagreed on how to raise the kids, how to spend time with each other and our families, and, of course, how to manage money.

These are problems that so many couples face, and we should have been more prepared. Our strategy for dealing with issues became increasingly dysfunctional. Ignore it. Don't talk about it. Let the tension build until we had a huge argument. Reconcile. Repeat. Between each stage of this cycle, we buried our frustrations under piles and piles of bad food.

Our pattern of making ill-informed, yet oddly romantic decisions continued when we decided we should try to have a baby. Kim's tubal ligation was a topic of discussion on our first date, and at the time, we felt good about our decision to devote all our resources to Adam and Emma. Despite all logic, we impulsively flew to North Carolina to the Chapel Hill Tubal Reversal Center. After meeting Dr. Gary Berger briefly, Kim underwent a procedure to have her fallopian tubes restored, then we got back on a plane and flew home the next day.

There were so many reasons why this was a bad idea. The procedure and travel were expensive, and we put it all on credit cards. We simply couldn't afford it, and we are still feeling the financial consequences of this choice. At the time, our weight was going up and up. In fact, Kim teetered on the edge of the cutoff weight for the surgery. They required a BMI of 30 or less for patients to be operated on in their freestanding facility, and her BMI was hovering around 29. We were sitting in a doctor's office in another state, hoping the scale would reveal a number low enough for the surgery to proceed. She made it, she had the operation, then we both flew home with a misguided but powerful sense that a baby would solve all our problems.

Over the months that we were trying to conceive, our focus remained on all the wrong things. We talked a lot about baby names, what the child might look like and all the family photos we would take, but we didn't talk at all about our ballooning weight, our dire financial situation or how we didn't truly want to raise another child. We were again putting a band-aid on our lives, trying to make ourselves happy with something that couldn't do that. I was caught up in the idea of having a kid that was a combination of both of us, and I thought the child's existence would somehow cement us as a real family, that it would create a link between me and Adam and Emma that didn't exist biologically.

I couldn't see in that moment that our family was as real as any family. We were living and loving together and solving problems the best way we knew how. Kim was caught up in the sentimental notion that giving me a baby would somehow make me happy and complete. She led herself to believe that another round of motherhood would give her a renewed purpose in life. Month after month, when we learned Kim wasn't pregnant, it was a bittersweet mix of disappointment and relief.

Eventually, we acknowledged that we didn't want another child enough to keep putting ourselves through the rollercoaster, and we made the decision that I would have a vasectomy to close that chapter of our lives. It was an empowering and honest choice, but also an ironic and costly way to realize we already had the family we wanted.

Our careers were also going through upheavals during this time that added to the stress in our marriage. I had been teaching for seven years when I met Kim. I enjoyed teaching, but I was starting to feel slightly trapped in the profession. My education degree qualified me to do nothing else. I decided to get a Master's degree in Counselor Education so I could have the option to leave the classroom and become a guidance counselor. I'm grateful for that choice because it led me to the same class that Kim was taking to complete her Master's in Higher Education, but ultimately, I didn't complete the degree as planned. The stability of remaining in the classroom was more appealing after taking on the responsibilities of a house and a family. I individualized my program, which basically means I took enough courses to earn a Master's degree that qualifies me to do...nothing else. Fortunately for me, my itch to leave teaching was temporary. I grew to love the work again despite its frustrations.

After our first married year of my 35-minute commute to the school I'd taught at when we met, I'd gotten a new job teaching 10 minutes from home and intended to remain in that district for the duration of my career. Kim had hoped to work at the University of Maine, which is also about 10 minutes away. We were working on a grand vision of setting up deep roots in the community, both of us making long-term career goals, picturing the kids finishing their public schooling without disruption and maybe going to UMaine as we had both done.

Fate threw us a curveball when my teaching position was eliminated after only two years due to budget cuts. I was terrified. I was the primary breadwinner for our family, and we could not survive without my income. I spent several months searching for a new job, applying for anything in a reasonable driving distance. I briefly considered cobbling together a full-time, though significantly smaller, salary by accepting a position as a half-time Ed Tech and substitute in a town 90 minutes north of our hometown. I also briefly accepted a job working in an alternative reading program in the state capital two hours away. I didn't even want to do this work, and the commute would have been a nightmare, but I felt like I had to do it to stave off financial ruin.

In a seemingly rare stroke of good fortune, I received an offer to teach English in a good paying school district in a town an hour from home. The offer came late in the summer, but in the nick of time before I signed a contract for the job I truly didn't want. I have now been in my current position for 12 years. I plan to retire from this district when the time comes, and I feel like I am meant to be there. However, the irony of leaving a stable position to avoid a commute and ending up with a longer one is not lost on me. The entire experience made me more worried than ever about our ability to make a decision that we wouldn't regret.

A constant but ever-changing theme in our lives during this time was Kim's efforts to launch a career of her own. Kim was a great student in high school with enormous potential. She went to the University of Maine on full academic scholarship with plans to become an English teacher. She's always loved teachers, so it's no surprise that she ultimately married one. Her teaching ambitions were interrupted when she got married while still in college and had a baby before graduation.

She dabbled in various jobs during her first marriage, including medical transcription and real estate. After her divorce, she went back to grad school to earn a Master's degree in Higher Education with a goal to do some kind of student services work. She took out significant student loans to finance her aspirations and support her children but believed wholeheartedly that it would pay off with a rewarding career.

When I met Kim, she was almost finished with her program. She was working with undergraduate students in campus activities and wanted to work with that population full time after graduation. This line of work seemed like a perfect fit. She has a strong appreciation for education and helping people figure out their strengths and weaknesses is a strong skill set for her. We expected that she would have a long career at UMaine as a career counselor.

When a position didn't materialize, she decided to return to school to earn a second Master's degree in Counseling in hopes of being certified as a guidance counselor. There seemed to be more job opportunities in the K-12 school system, plus there was the congruence with my teaching calendar if she ended up having summers off. Although taking out more student loans on top of all our other debt was a gamble, we decided it would pay off in the long run. Toward the end of that program, she had to make a choice to focus on school counseling or mental health counseling, and she chose to go with a mental health focus, doing a year-long unpaid internship with teen parents in a school setting. She loved that job, but debt climbed astronomically as she put expensive gas on a credit card to commute to a job that paid nothing.

Kim got her conditional license as a mental health counselor, but the profession was fraught with uncertainty and poor working conditions. After doing home-based work with families and school-based work with younger children for a few years, she felt burned out. Her attention returned to college career counseling, but the time that had passed since earning her Higher Ed degree made it more difficult to compete for those positions.

Along the way, Kim worked at home as a medical transcriptionist to help make ends meet, but she remained unsatisfied with her failure to jumpstart a meaningful career. Along with our ongoing need for more income, she wanted a path that would make feel like she was achieving her higher purpose. I was also frustrated by the financial pressures, along with a strong desire for Kim to find the niche that would make her happy.

During all these upheavals, our lack of communication and poor coping skills continued to negatively impact our marriage. We were fighting more often and our responses to the stressors in our lives made the situation worse instead of better. I tended to shut down and go silent. Kim would leave the house with the kids to escape the tension. Through it all, food remained our primary source of entertainment and our most reliable outlet. I wonder now what people were thinking about us during those years. The social contract demands that we remain silent about weight gain, but when a couple gains over 200 pounds, it does not go unnoticed. It was an embarrassing, frustrating, and deeply unhappy time in our lives.

Ryan: Hiding in Plain Sight

Being fat is a lot like being Bigfoot. You know the famous still shot of Bigfoot from the Patterson-Gimlin video footage? The one where the beast is walking towards the woods, looking over its shoulder at the photographer as it retreats into the woods? I used to joke that I resembled that image in every picture taken of me from 2008 to 2014. I was definitely an elusive photo subject, but the occasional photographic evidence of my existence showed an unhappy and mostly uncooperative subject. As my weight continued to climb, I became more and more isolated and avoidant.

I became more socially awkward than ever, always anxious that I would run into someone who had witnessed my big weight loss and would instantly recognize me for the colossal hypocrite that I was. I was most comfortable when invisible, even when hiding in plain sight. If I saw a familiar face in public, I would turn in the opposite direction and hope to remain unnoticed.

I went to great lengths to remain detached from life and avoid any interaction that would make me feel like I was under scrutiny for gaining so much weight. We stayed home most of the time and didn't socialize much with other people. Our lives revolved around endless eating and watching TV. I was convinced I was dragging Kim down with me. I believed that I had somehow pulled a bait and switch on her, tricking her into believing I was a healthy man only to reveal that I was as messed up as ever. I worried that Kim used food to deal with the disappointment of being married to me.

My day-to-day mood was dominated by one emotion: anger. I was mad at myself for allowing all my hard work to go up in smoke. I was mad that I looked like a failure to all the people who applauded when I lost the weight before. I was mad that getting married and having a family didn't fix all my problems. I was a beast to live with.

I was so consumed with burying myself under food that I wasn't really available to anyone or anything else. I put on a socially acceptable front to the outside world, but at home, I was mostly sullen and silent. I often felt like I was an outsider at home, physically present but not truly part of the family. I told Kim that it sometimes felt like my only function in the household was to go to work and bring home a paycheck. I saw myself as separate from Kim and the kids, and as a result, I pulled further away.

I was inwardly fuming all the time about my failure to be the husband and stepfather I had set out to be. When Kim and I got married, I believed that being fat and unhappy was part of the past, and I was on the road to something so much better. The sobering reality that life was not that easy, and the fact that I had ended up where I started really broke me. It was like the original weight loss was just a tease to show me that the good things in life were meant for other people, but not for me. I can look back on it now and see that I was still a very lucky man. I had a supportive and loving wife and two amazing step-kids. I had it all, but I couldn't see it at the time.

It was a dark time for me, but I didn't lose all hope. I remained a curious, if jealous, observer of people, interested in being more connected to life. I thought I would be happier if I could just lose weight, so I continued to search for the all-mighty answer to being fat. I listened to podcasts, watched YouTube videos and read blogs in my ongoing search for THE THING that would solve my weight problem once and for all.

I tried Weight Watchers a couple times, the online version, even losing 25 pounds on the plan. At first, their plan worked well for me. I like clarity and the rules around WW points seemed easy to follow, but only for a few months. I started lying to myself, fudging the numbers, then canceled the program altogether. I tried using online nutrition counters to track calories and workouts. I experimented with meal replacement shakes, took another look at veganism, attempted to Couch to 5k. You name it, I either tried it or made a half-hearted plan to try it. What I didn't realize is that I was focused on fixing the symptom instead of dealing with the real cause of my unhappiness, and while I was wasting time with that, I was ignoring real consequences to my health.

Kim: Fat Mom

At some moment that I can't pinpoint, I just gave up. I ate what I wanted - more than I wanted - and in the process, I gained over 80 pounds in less than five years' time. My mid-to-late 30's were characterized by struggle: trying unsuccessfully to conceive, numerous disappointing, dead-end career paths, and ever-present sugar cravings that plagued my days. I felt beaten down by worrying and anxiety, by the tricks it seemed life had played, and I just didn't have it in me to fight anymore. The image of my defeat looks like this: me sitting alone in my car, stuffing something from a paper bag into my face, feeling numb and sad, then tossing the evidence into a trash can and heading to pick up my kids. That was a daily occurrence for a long time.

I didn't diet during those years of rapid gain. Weight Watchers had given me a classic case of decision fatigue, agonizing about how to spread out my points and eat frequent tiny snacks that left me ravenous. Jenny Craig sucked the joy out of my days with overpriced food that was barely edible. Every new diet that came down the pike, every eating-related suggestion from Ryan, all were met with a sigh and an eye roll from me. I was tired of struggling with rigid diet rules, so I made the decision that not trying was better than trying and failing.

This all related back to the shame-driven perfectionism that had been with me since childhood. Be perfect, it said, or you just aren't good enough. I was an excellent test-taker, but I can recall leaving a question blank when I was unsure because anything was better than writing the wrong answer. When it came to weight, I just couldn't tolerate what felt like another way to fail in life. I told myself not to be vain. I figured some people were just meant to be heavy; certainly, you can look around and see them everywhere.

I'd never been particularly girly or fancy, but I stopped even my basic routine of hair styling or putting on mascara or lip gloss. I cut my hair in a short, low-maintenance style, and started wearing my glasses instead of contact lenses. None of these are bad things, but looking back, they are signals of an internal shift. Not caring about my appearance was part of not caring about myself at all.

My dear friend Felicia has cut my hair for nearly a decade, still does, so she has been privy to each stage of my evolution. She and I now laugh about my "mini bang phase," but she can also speak solemnly to what it was like to watch me go through years where I would not meet my own eye in the mirror. I so appreciate her perspective as she describes how I've changed, most recently for the better.

In 2012, I attended my 20th high school class reunion. I'm still proud of the fact that despite weight gain of nearly 100 pounds since the day of our graduation, I pushed myself to attend this event. I had attended my 10th reunion newly divorced with my head held high, then attended my 20th with a huge weight gain but still with my head held high. This is the resilience that carried me through the hardest parts of my journey, the knowledge that I'm a good, kind person with a lot to offer. I wasn't proud of how I looked, but I wanted to see and interact with my classmates.

The night of the reunion was a hot, humid evening with temps hovering in the high 80s as night fell. Unfortunately, the venue was not air-conditioned. I'd poured myself into Spanx covered by a blouse and gauchos made of a nylon blend. I can still remember how sweaty I was, and how I struggled to wrestle myself back into the layers of damp, suffocating fabric after using the restroom. It was mortifying. Even though I was in the privacy of a bathroom stall, I was keenly aware that most of my high school classmates were mere feet away laughing, dancing and (I believed) enjoying the freedom I wanted so badly. Almost nothing about my life had turned out the way I'd imagined when we were graduating 20 years earlier, and my weight was the biggest, most obvious part of it.

When the pictures from the event surfaced, I was mortified at how my big I looked, my makeup threatening to sweat off my face. I sullenly remarked that I looked like Mimi from the Drew Carey show. I hated how I looked and was horrified by my careening weight gain, but I had no idea what to do differently, so I kept doing exactly what I had been doing, and I continued to gain.

As I approached my 40th birthday (a cliched but common time to take stock of one's life), I was completely beaten down. What was I thinking day to day? I can't be totally sure, but it was along the lines of this: I'd had my chance to succeed in terms of weight, health, and career, and I'd blown it all. This was worse than the "honor student turned broke divorcee" pity party; I genuinely believed that at the relatively young age of 40, I'd missed the boat of life completely.

It wasn't t about me anymore; it was about my kids and passing the torch, hoping they'd be happier than I'd managed to be. Secretly, I was terrified of what would happen when my kids left the nest, leaving me alone with my eating and my feelings of failure. Like so many ironies of weight gain, the more afraid I felt of being left behind, the more I ate and the more my weight swelled.

During this same era of my life, my grandmother passed away at age 95. She and I were very close, and not even in a spend-lots-of-time-together way, but in a deeper way than that. I was strongly attached to her from childhood on. My earliest memories are of being gathered up in her soft, powdery embrace. She was the person who always made me feel special and beautiful, no matter how many failures I experienced or how much weight I gained.

Though she lived a long, healthy life and died essentially of old age, her passing shook me in the way some people describe when they lose both parents. I felt orphaned, vulnerable in the world in a way I hadn't felt before. For several weeks following her death, my grief was an active, time-consuming and energy-sapping process that filled my days. I had always been one to cry easily, but never before had I cried every single day for a month in a row.

Because I worked at home on my own schedule, I was available to complete those practical tasks of dealing with a loved one's death. Gram had inhabited her house on Elm Street for 66 years and her essence was on and in every inch of it. Just stepping up into her kitchen, the wave of nostalgia was dizzying and nearly knocked me backward. I felt like a little girl again, yet there was no Gram wiping her hands on her apron.

The house was, as they say, jammed to the gills. She had saved everything from the sentimental to the silly. I spent hours sorting through photos and trinkets. There were boxes of holiday decorations, long unused. There were empty mayonnaise jars and margarine containers, washed and ready to be filled with something else. She had legitimate antiques stacked in the cellar, covered in cobwebs. Whether it was Depression-era frugality or an undiagnosed case of hoarding disorder, she left a jam-packed house that was going to take sweat and tears to clean out for the new owners.

An upstairs closet contained my father's old clothes, eyeglasses, and college textbooks from the 1960s. My aunt's bedroom had vintage prom dresses and her graduation cap and gown. My grandfather's dresser in their bedroom was still full, his wallet and pocket knife neatly placed in the top drawer, though he had died a quarter-century earlier. In the bathroom, she had his combs and a half-used tube of Brylcreem, never discarded.

She had old family Bibles and dozens of yellowed obituaries clipped from the newspaper. She kept every honor roll listing that mentioned me; she even had faded purple mimeographed newsletters about my preschool-era accomplishments. Most touching was finding all the pictures and drawings she kept from Adam and Emma. She loved us so, and though we knew it, touching all those things made it real in a new way.

Over those weeks, I ritualistically stood at her kitchen sink looking out the window, trying to calculate in my head how many times she might have stood in that exact spot, looking out at those exact trees. 66 years is 24,000 days, and she never had an automatic dishwasher, so it is possible she stood there washing dishes upwards of 80,000 times. It was deeply comforting to stand there and feel her presence with me.

44

Likewise, I spent many hours just sitting in her rocking chair. Her emery boards and her hand cream were on the side table where she left them. Her book rested with a bookmark stuck at a spot it would never move from. I sat with my eyes closed, listening to the clock on her wall tick, wishing I could slow or freeze it, just linger in this space where she had been. Soon the house would be sold and quickly renovated, and I knew that the work I was doing was the best way to keep moving. It was also to honor Gram, who had been unable in life to part with all these things.

I packed up the items filling that sweet little house from attic to basement, every drawer, every cabinet, every closet. I soaked up each bit of those final days spent in what had been my personal oasis of tranquility. Most days, I was there alone while the kids were at school and Ryan was at work. I moved from room to room openly weeping, grief washing over me in wave after wave. It was strangely familiar to be there with the sights, sounds and smells I knew, but also profoundly different. Gram was not here anymore, and she never would be again. It felt like something inside me was shifting and changing, and I look back now and realize I needed my world to be rocked that hard.

I wish I could say I went home and made positive changes immediately, but I wallowed for many months to come. At first, Gram's death significantly intensified my use of sugary, starchy food as an outlet. A memory from the days following her death is going with my sister Mary to get Chinese takeout after the funeral. While the fortune cookie wisdom about making sure to serve others was a poignant reminder of how Gram lived (the little slip of paper is still on my fridge), drowning my sorrow in a pile of oily noodles and MSG didn't help anything. My behavior was more than appropriate comfort eating.

My food struggles escalated as I careened from one binge to the next through an entire year of grieving. My consumption of wine increased from 1-2 glasses a week to 1-2 glasses a night. About a year after Gram died, in the fall of 2014, Ryan's weight was dropping and mine was at its all-time high. I can never remember the exact number, but it was either 237 or 243. I tend to say 240 as a good round estimate. Most of the "before" pictures that I have shared online during this IF journey came from that phase.

Workwise, after my stint in the field of mental health burned me out, I had gone into full retreat mode. This is truly how I look back on it, that I packed up my therapy workbooks and inspirational posters and dejectedly went home. I spent a couple years cobbling together an income by teaching at the community college during the day and doing transcription wherever I could find a few spare hours. Teaching was something I had dreamed of doing for a long time, but the development didn't make me happy. Standing in front of the classroom, I shuddered at the image I knew they were seeing.

I was larger than I'd ever been, far heavier than during my pregnancies. I was heavy enough that my gait had slowed, ever-so-slightly rocking back and forth to accommodate my extra weight. There was aching in my knees after extended walking or standing, and whichever side I slept on at night, I woke with a sore hip on that side. Certainly if I rushed to class because I couldn't find a parking spot, students would see me flushed and trying to conceal that I was breathing heavily. I made too many self-deprecating comments and jokes about my weight and my eating. I had an almost compulsive need to make sure people knew that I was aware of how fat I was. I felt like I needed to bring up the subject out loud lest they think I didn't know.

While I did enjoy interacting with students on campus, ultimately the teaching was not what I needed. I was an adjunct faculty member with little prospect of becoming full-time, so each semester I hung in at it was prolonging the inevitable question of what to be "when I grew up." Emma was reaching high school age and the empty nest loomed. Though teaching got me out of the house a few times a week, I spent most of my time at home typing, which was isolating and a recipe for unsupervised eating. I still needed to find a cohesive career direction to move in.

From my vantage point now, being a size 4 and often unable to find clothing SMALL enough in stores, I shake my head to recall the nightmare that was shopping during my heaviest years. I stopped going into certain stores at all or only went into them when trailing around behind Emma. I didn't even bother looking much at the clothes she bought. I know many mothers cannot share clothing with their teenage daughters, but I had over 100 pounds on mine, so we couldn't even share a sweater or jacket. I was literally twice her size.

Emma attended a K-8 school and had the same circle of friends from the time she was in primary grades. It's difficult to explain how I felt about being the largest one when the mothers gathered. I think I closed myself off to thinking about or caring too much about it. Emma was slim and pretty, and I was frequently given compliments on her appearance by strangers. For whatever reason, this helped bolster my confidence, knowing that somehow even though I'd failed to maintain my health or appearance, I had made a beautiful daughter. The mind does so many things to protect us from psychological pain.

When my size reached its peak, I limited shopping to the plus section of a big-box store like Walmart and K-Mart. I hated most of the bright-colored, sequined tops, but I managed to locate enough muted colors and subtle prints to dress myself and function in the world every day. There was no need for anything to be fitted or look good at that point. I didn't have any clothes I can say I liked, though my favorites were the ones that were most comfortable. I avoided changing rooms with their mirrored walls and bought things by eyeballing them with a nod of yeah, that's huge enough, that'll do.

At my heaviest, I went through a phase of buying a specific style of Lee jeans. I remember having a couple pair in size 18W and, at some point, instinctively knowing they were getting tight and buying a couple pair in size 20W. Our local K-Mart has since gone out of business, but I have clear memories of that dingy, run-down store, me tossing a bigger pair of jeans in my cart like I was picking up extra toilet paper. I had no idea what I really looked like; we did not even have a full-length mirror in our home during those years. I felt as disconnected from my body as I had at age 10, standing on the sidelines on field day. I felt as disconnected from my body as I had at age 22, in the throes of painful induced labor, unable to push my baby boy into the world. My body was just a thing to move my head from place to place.

I now see women from the body positive movement who wear incredibly attractive, nicely accessorized outfits at sizes as large as and even larger than I was. I wish I could've been in that place, but my weight was a reflection of my inner struggle of feeling unworthy. I didn't enjoy a single day of loving my body or feeling confident and attractive when I was at my heaviest.

Eventually, I purchased a single pair of those Riders by Lee jeans in size 22W, the largest I ever owned, a pair I would thankfully not need for long. Incidentally, I still own those jeans today; they are in like-new condition, but I keep them to hold up and remember that there was a day when I walked around filling them. Today, it is not painful to look at them, because I now have the mental and physical tools to avoid ever needing to wear them again.

Ryan: Primal Directions

By the summer of 2014, my weight reached an all-time high. I didn't even pretend to care about carb counts and hadn't tested my blood sugar in years.   My previous weight loss had essentially "cured" my diabetes, so I told myself that I had plenty of time to turn it around, but I knew it was a lie.

Intellectually, I knew that regaining so much body fat made it not only possible but likely that my blood sugar was running high. I was well-educated about the dangers of the disease but choosing to keep my head in the sand. Emotionally, I just wasn't ready to act on it. I was stuck in a long-standing pattern of getting through each day by eating and telling myself that I would lose the weight soon. Eventually, just like in 2001 when I received the initial diagnosis, the fear of the serious consequences of out of control blood sugar compelled me to have a blood test.

When my doctor's office left me a voicemail, I called back knowing what she was going to say but naively clinging to hope that I had dodged a bullet. I was told very matter-of-factly that my fasting blood sugar and A1c were too high, and with those words, I was transported back to 2001. I felt the same emotions I had the first time - scared, confused, and above all frustrated that I had allowed myself to arrive at this point again. In the moment though, I asked for a prescription for testing supplies and braced myself to get back on the diabetes train.

The initial days and weeks of readjusting to the routines of treating diabetes were rough. I struggled emotionally with the reality of testing again and a high number felt like a punch in the gut. Although I knew it would take time to bring the numbers down, I felt like a complete failure when the transition was not immediate. I decided to count carbs to control my blood sugar, the same method that I used the first time, but my body didn't respond in the same way.   The number of carbs that produced a good result years earlier was now yielding a number higher than I wanted. My doctor offered a referral to a diabetes educator, but I rejected the idea. I was

49

determined to radically alter my lifestyle again but in a completely different direction.

I had been flirting with the Paleo/Primal diet for a while before I was re-diagnosed. I had the same intense curiosity that I felt for vegetarianism years before, and just like before, I became convinced that it was the best way for me to take off weight and treat my diabetes. The irony of that decision is not lost on me.

In many ways, the Paleo way of eating is the polar opposite of the vegetarian diet that I successfully used before. I lost 120 pounds eating a mostly vegetarian diet that emphasized plants and grains, essentially a high carb low-fat diet. I did maintain a specific carb allotment for each meal and snack, but I ate often, believing that a steady influx of healthy carbs throughout the day was the ideal way to control weight and blood sugar. It worked, too, until I stopped eating that way and regained it all.

The Paleo diet, on the other hand, is a high-fat low carb diet that emphasizes meat, vegetables and fats while shunning carbs, particularly simple carbs like bread, potatoes and desserts. Proponents of the Paleo diet claimed that you need to eat less often because protein and fat are more satisfying.

In light of this paradox, I don't completely understand why this new plan appealed to me so much. The tide was turning in the court of public opinion towards low-carb eating with a resurgence of the Atkins diet and various other books on the market. I was always susceptible to the "the diet of the moment", but this seemed to be different somehow. There was more information coming out about the insulin theory and metabolic syndrome and evolutionary theories about the optimal human diet, but if I'm being honest, it was the caveman schtick that really reeled me in. Many marketers of Paleo geared their programs to men, suggesting that this way of eating was a return to our ancient roots, a pathway to more muscle, vitality, and longevity. The superficial AND the scientific claims spoke to me, and I jumped in with both feet.

It worked. The weight again came off steadily though my day-to-day life was very different. I was eating eggs, bacon and Greek yogurt for breakfast, and mostly meat and vegetables for lunch and dinner. It felt liberating to eat butter, olive oil, and fatty meat again while losing weight. I didn't really miss eating carbs, in part because I was willing to occasionally cheat to have a piece of birthday cake or something equally special.

Paleo enthusiasts have particular guidelines about exercise but place greater value on food type and quality. This was great for me, especially at the beginning, since I was too heavy to enjoy high-intensity exercise safely. I started walking a lot more, and as I became leaner, I experimented with high-intensity interval training, but I can't attribute much of the weight loss to it.

History repeated itself in a number of ways as I lost the weight again. I experienced all the milestones again. At approximately the 40 pounds lost mark, friends and colleagues started to compliment me and ask what I was doing. I melted out of my clothes and had to buy new stuff. I started feeling more comfortable and confident. More importantly, my health markers all improved dramatically. My fasting blood sugar and A1c numbers were soon in the exceptional range. I felt like high-fat low carb eating was the permanent solution to my weight issues.

One major difference during this round of weight loss was my relationship with Kim. I was losing weight, but she was not. She was supportive of my eating, but she was not interested in doing the same. We were no longer partners in crime with our co-dependent eating patterns. This was uncharted territory for our marriage.

Kim: The Carbohydrate Addict's Diet

I'll always remember that 2014 phone call about Ryan's high blood sugar and his quick decision to turn his health around by changing his eating dramatically. It was both inspiring and discouraging for me. It's been a long-standing theme in our marriage that I feel inferior to Ryan's ability to "adult" - he is more consistent, more organized, and has systems in place for keeping track of things and getting stuff done. Of course, I have many strengths he does not, namely my spontaneity and outbursts of enthusiastic energy, but my feelings of shame intensified as he swiftly brought his eating under control.

If I'm being honest, it was difficult for me to be happy for him when his rapid weight loss results became apparent. Envy is such a strong, negative emotion in the realm of people who struggle with their weight; it's been an especially hurtful part of my weight-loss success to perceive others as more envious of than happy for me, but I totally understand it and as I just confessed, I've been there myself.

Of course, with the cheap, knee-jerk jealousy stripped away, I was relieved that Ryan had averted a full-blown diabetic crisis. Because of his family history, I knew diabetes could have caused numerous medical complications if he hadn't taken swift action. However, it felt like a lot of pressure on me as the remaining heavy spouse. For the first time since the day we met, I outweighed him. Part of our image all along was that I was a couple inches shorter and a few pounds lighter. Now, there was this unbalanced phase I refer to as the "Jack Sprat and his wife" chapter. I saw us in photographs and it just seemed wrong that I was fat and he wasn't. I inwardly whined, no fair, you are making me look fatter by being so much thinner!

Couples come in all shapes and sizes, but our thing from the beginning had been to stay in the same general category. Our time together had revolved around going out like predators on a hunt, rounding up then devouring our favorite junk foods; it felt like part of our bond. A mix of negative emotions swirled at the idea that he might be leaving me behind for good. For several months as Ryan's weight dropped, I kept eating the same way I'd eaten for years, stubborn but scared about what it all meant. Was I waiting for a sign? I'm not sure if I was, but one was on its way.

In the spring of 2015, as Ryan was reaching his goal weight, I spun my transcription skills into a job as a medical scribe for a busy surgeon, taking real-time dictation into electronic medical record software. I accepted the position not understanding how it would change my life beyond a steady paycheck. In those early months, Dr. Starks taught me about the process of examining and assessing the patient in front of you, about delivering high-quality, personalized care. Being a quiet witness to his encounters with patients was a spiritual experience that it is difficult to describe, but suffice it to say, it changed me. I saw pain, illness, health, love, trust and a myriad of critical pieces of the human experience up close in ways that deepened my gratitude and my faith in humanity.

That's a high level of 'woo', but more practically speaking, getting out of the house and into the world of work made me think about my health and my massive weight. After hiding in plain sight for years, I found myself in an office full of women talking of things like a new dress for an upcoming wedding or getting ready for bathing suit season. I also got to know Amy, our office manager, who is an incredibly positive, encouraging person who reminded me of my unique gifts. I will always be grateful to Amy for helping me believe in my own potential. It was another ingredient in the transformation I was about to undergo.

As an obese medical scribe, I felt especially attuned to those patients who were dealing with significant medical conditions related to obesity or complications stemming from gastric bypass surgery. Though I had never consciously considered gastric bypass (again, destined to be fat had become a self-fulfilling prophecy), I decided to do something to prevent ever arriving at the threshold of weight-loss surgery. While I do not judge it as a personal decision some make, I feel strongly about my stomach and intestines, with all of their inherent abilities to absorb nutrition, staying intact if humanly possible.

Maybe it was the confidence from succeeding in a brand-new role Dr. Starks and I had invented together - he had never used a scribe and there was no formal training offered when I was hired. Maybe it was divine intervention - I often look back on this time in my life, the spring/summer of 2015, and say my grandmother pulled some strings from above for me. Whatever made the stars align, I pushed past the fear of failing that held me back from adopting the last several weight-loss plans Ryan had tried. I arrived once again at the familiar old "Monday morning of my new diet" moment with both apprehension and excitement.

Because I'd taken off some weight by restricting carbs in the past, I went back to my own version of the Heller's Carb Addict's Diet (CAD). For me, this meant a couple cups of coffee with cream through the morning hours, a low-carb lunch of salad with protein, and whatever I wanted for dinner, consumed within a one-hour span. This usually meant a dinner of pasta, pizza or breaded chicken. The sugar cravings were intense at first, but ultimately, the less sugar I ate, the better that part got. Though I was eating more salad, I was still not wild for vegetables and I loved being "allowed" a daily dessert like ice cream or pastries. I still tell people (as does Gin) that the CAD can be a reasonable stepping stone to intermittent fasting. In essence, what I was doing during those months was a form of IF with dirty fasts due to all the coffee with cream.

Weight came off steadily because even with a relative lack of nutrient-dense whole food, I was eating far less than I had before implementing the plan. From mid-2015 to early 2016, I lost 50-something pounds over about a 9-month span. I had gone from 240 to about 185, which was finally "One-derland", or finally being back in the 100s. It also took me from size 22W back down to a size 14, which was on the cusp of being able to shop in the non-plus-sized section. I was still heavier than I had been when Ryan and I met, but I felt normal again (the average American woman, they say, is a size 14).

With my out-of-control sugar binges reined in to a controlled level, I felt healthier than I had in a long time. I didn't feel gorgeous, but I was pleased about the change in my appearance, especially because I had given up for so long on ever getting below 200 pounds. I'm sure on some level I intended to follow the Carb Addict's plan long term for maintenance, but looking back, my behavior said that I was happily moving out of diet mode and back to so-called regular eating.

Ryan: Falling off the Wagon

As Kim lost weight, and we entered a new phase in which we were both thinner, eating together remained a challenge. Our styles were not completely incompatible, but we were not on the same page either. I was particularly militant about following my Paleo-style rules. I was motivated in large part by my desire to control my blood sugar and improve my overall health, which was a positive development, but it also meant my day-to-day eating was rigidly structured and, frankly, pretty boring.

I didn't like to eat at restaurants or accept dinner invitations from others because I was afraid there wouldn't be anything I would want to eat. I would sometimes make concessions for special occasions, but if I deviated from my plan too much or too often, I would struggle with feelings of failure and worry about gaining weight. I generally found it easier to eat at home and to eat a fairly narrow range of meals, so I stuck to those patterns tightly.

Kim's plan allowed her to eat carbs, but only for dinner, which was typically the only meal we were eating together. Kim had primary responsibility for meal planning and preparation at that point, and I'm certain my ways made the process more difficult. She has always been a person who takes care of the people she loves, so she tried hard to make it all work. She would cook a chicken and rice meal, but I would skip the rice and add extra vegetables. I would eat big bowls or meat sauce with cheese while she added spaghetti. Or she might make hamburgers, but I would refuse to eat the bun.

Of course, I was also eating lunch. Kim would make extra protein at dinner, so I could pack meals to take to work. She was also having dessert every night. I was shunning sugar most of the time, so I would start washing dishes while she was finishing her meal. Some of these differences may seem insignificant, but overall it made grocery shopping, meal planning and even the meal itself more of a tedious chore than the joy eating is supposed to be.

Despite the ongoing negotiations around food, our marriage improved in a lot of ways. We were more content with ourselves, and that translated into being happier together. We were physically healthier and more fit than we had been in a long time, so we were spending more quality time together, getting more active and tentatively introducing new things and people into our lives.

The children were older and more independent, and we were more certain than ever about our decision to not have a baby. My teaching career was going well, and I had become the head of my department. Kim was enjoying her new work as a medical scribe and feeling a sense of purpose and higher calling that she had been seeking for a long time.

Ironically, as Kim and I grew happier, we also began to gradually loosen the reins on our new eating habits. It was eerily familiar to the first couple of years of married life when controlling our food intake was less important than just being together and experiencing life. Even though I had literally regained 120 pounds once before, I still somehow believed that this time was different, that if I changed the way I was eating it would have no consequence.

I began to eat "off plan" more and more often, always figuring that I would get back on track tomorrow. My occasional indulgences for birthdays or holidays became increasingly random and frequent. Kim was finding herself on an equally slippery slope. Her way of eating allowed her to have carbs every night, but her meals were becoming larger and more unbalanced, particularly her desserts.

We also began drifting into old patterns of enabling each other, giving each permission to make unhealthy choices. The weight began to creep back on. Another ritual that fueled our regain was weekly brunch after church. We loved everything about it. It gave us a special opportunity to focus on each other, to talk about the sermon we just heard and to discuss the week ahead. Of course, it was mostly about the food. Carbs like pancakes and waffles have always been Kim's kryptonite, and it wasn't long before my pledges to eat bacon and eggs were overridden by my desire to eat those foods with her.

By June of 2017, we had regained about 40 pounds between us. We were both disappointed in ourselves and desperate to stop the runaway train and take the weight off. We were telling ourselves that we just needed to summon the willpower to resume our plans and stick to the rules that helped us lose the weight instead of figuring out why those rules were so hard to follow.

As our daughter's high school graduation approached, we were distracted by thoughts of what clothes we could fit into and dreading the inevitable photos. We were so proud of Emma, and her graduation weekend was special, but those photos do tell another tale. Behind our smiles, you can see the anxiety of being the object of attention, even though Emma was the star of the day.

You can see how physically uncomfortable we were, squeezed into clothes that fit well a few months before. We didn't know then that a lifestyle that truly works should be sustainable and not a constant battle. We probably wouldn't have believed such a thing exists, but we were about to experience a way of eating that would take our lives in a bold new direction.

Kim: Magical Thinking

A thousand psychology books have been written about the lies we tell and the ways we delude ourselves. It is amazing how magical thinking takes over the human brain. Somehow by the summer of 2016, I decided weight loss mode was over and I could eat what I wanted "within reason", whatever that means. I was spending more time in nature and feeling more spiritually centered and calm than ever. I wanted to focus my energy on the larger meaning of life, not obsessing over food. I told myself that food was a small and petty issue and dwelling on it was getting in the way of my ability to enjoy my life, as my grandmother had urged me to do. I felt an unfamiliar steady contentment, the first glimmer that I was shedding my old identity of being marked for struggle, but the war was far from over.

The problem was that the more I ignored the plan I was supposed to be on, the more extraneous noshing I did. I had not counted calories specifically as part of the CAD, so I'm not sure how my daily calorie count was increasing. I know I was definitely taking more liberties. I wonder now if people noticed that I had fallen off the wagon, but ultimately, I understand that people are too busy with their own lives to care if a friend or co-worker puts on a few pounds. Those who notice are likely too polite to ask you whether you realize how badly you are sabotaging yourself left and right.

During this time, Dr. Starks sold his private practice to a small community hospital….one with a full-service cafeteria! We packed up and moved our office across town. Suddenly gone were the days when I could bring my Mason jar of spinach, peppers, and vinaigrette and be insulated from temptation. Pizza, sandwiches, muffins, and cookies quickly became workday staples.

Ryan and I started going to church, then out to big Sunday brunches. Gorging on carbs felt familiar in a guilty but strangely pleasant way. The biggest sign of having slipped all the way off plan was the resumption of my late-night waffles or Toaster Strudels. During the school year, Ryan goes to bed much earlier than I, and it was a long-time pattern for me to eat sweets once he'd gone to bed. I again found myself eating plates of Eggos drowned in butter, syrup and melting chocolate chips after 9:00 PM on a nightly basis.

I was eating and enjoying, in total denial about the consequences, happy in my job and pleased that Ryan was doing well overall. I didn't worry much about his expanding carb intake or what that might be doing to his blood sugar, either. In retrospect, in addition to the creeping weight gain, I did not feel genuinely good during this time. Physically, I was right back to craving sugar all day long. Mentally, I was disappointed that I seemed to be failing yet-again to be a person who could "eat normally." My Instagram account is filled with pictures from those days, things like me holding up giant cookies with captions like "Oops, I did it again" and other attempts to use humor as a defense mechanism.

As the spring of 2017 rolled around, I faced yet-another dreaded milestone - Emma's high school graduation. Yes, the empty-nest implications were there, but I am talking about the fear of what to wear for those group family photos that would be taken. A standout theme from my Fat Mom Chronicles was that of graduations, and I'll recap it here: our kids attended a small K-8 community school where eighth-grade graduation is a big celebration, so I'd already endured two eighth-grade graduations, Adam's high school graduation plus his community college graduation as events at which to come up with something appropriate to wear. Those ceremonies took place in 2010, 2013, 2014 and 2016. Each subsequent event involved my weight swelling from the previous one.

At each of the first three, I had worn pants and a plus-sized top, feeling that wearing a dress was something I'd do when I took the weight off. I always believed (with no plan for how it would happen) that all the weight would be released eventually. When we arrived at Adam's college graduation in 2016, right after I lost 50 pounds doing my Carb Addict's plan, I bought a dress. I think it was a size 14, and though I didn't love it, wearing a dress was a triumph in itself. I fantasized about being in a size 12 by the time the next graduation ceremony rolled around a year later.

Unfortunately, as Emma's graduation loomed, instead of shopping for that dream dress I'd be proud to wear, I was struggling with re-gaining weight. Instead of getting into that long-awaited size 12, I was back to trying on 16s. In the weeks before school ended, Emma and I took our spring mother-daughter shopping trip, a beloved tradition, driving south to the bigger city of Portland two hours away and staying in a hotel. Over the years, it was also a time that was food-focused, as she came to love coffee shops and pastries as much as I did. We had such a good time on those trips, listening to music, eating, and shopping.

The Spring 2017 trip was heavily focused on trying on dresses because graduation was nearing. I have memories of carrying piles of hangers into a shared dressing room with my slender daughter. Everything she tried looked beautiful; everything I tried fit wrong. I felt frumpy and uncomfortable. The dress I bought was a size 14 and I tried to tell myself that hey, three years earlier, I was a 22W, so that's progress! I scolded myself for not being happier, not feeling grateful that I'd had the relative success I did.

Yet looking back, I did not feel calm or in control; I was terrified of gaining back every pound. I worried whether my creeping gain would make the dress too small within the few weeks between the purchase and the ceremony. It felt like I was going backward, and I felt totally desperate for a new plan. Desperation clouded what was supposed to be a happy, albeit stressful, time.

I spent a couple weeks trying to rein in my carb intake on my own, but every day I seemed to fail. Ryan was extra supportive as he witnessed my floundering, saying to me, "You know what worked for you. You just need to get back there." I heard him, I knew there was truth to what he was saying, but I could not seem to do it. Was the stress of the looming empty nest overwhelming me? I just know I had strong carb cravings and seemingly no resistance to the daily temptations I faced.

Every day was a new excuse to just have a panini at lunch (oh, the one with the pesto mayo, that one isn't offered often) or a gigantic cookie with my afternoon coffee (it has been a hard day and a starch/sugar rush will soothe). It is challenging to feel a sense of agency in your world when a turkey sandwich has more power than you do. My work clothes, newly purchased since my weight loss, were all becoming tight and uncomfortable. I was back to having pants that technically fit, but I would look at them in the morning and decide against them, knowing how restrictive they would feel.

There are photographs of me and my coworkers dressed up for a teambuilding day in May 2017, all wearing costumes based on the movie Grease. I wore Spanx under my pants, and in the pictures, you can see a visible indentation where the Spanx were cutting into my flesh, fat spilling out underneath them. I was embarrassed and increasingly, I felt panicked about getting into that dress. At least I cared; at least I wasn't giving in to defeat. Unfortunately, I was all over the place with my attempts to rein it in.

I tried canned shakes, an entire case of which went to waste after realizing I hate the taste of stevia. I bought a blender bottle and protein powder to make smoothies as a meal substitute. I contemplated joining a gym even though exercise had never played a big role in my successful weight loss efforts in the past. I prayed for something that would give me control of my life and health, something that would make me feel I was more powerful than these sugar cravings that dominated my days. There just had to be something out there that would give me freedom from and with food.

Ryan: Flirting with Fasting

I first heard about intermittent fasting years ago before I lost weight with low carb eating. When I was at my heaviest, I was constantly reading about diet trends and plans. I even tried most of them for a day or two. Like so many people who struggle with weight, I was convinced that if I could find just the right book, website or blog, all my problems would be solved.

I came across Dr. Bert Herring's book *The Fast 5 Diet* during a routine Google search. I was impressed that Dr. Herring was offering his book for free and that he seemed to be motivated by nothing more than wanting people to benefit from the information. I read it in one sitting and was immediately conflicted.

On the one hand, his explanation of limbic versus somatic hunger really resonated with me. I was very familiar with the reptilian part of my brain driving me to eat food that I didn't truly want or need, and I liked the promise of a solution that was deceptively simple, just eat your calories for the day in a 5-hour eating window. On the other hand, the simplicity that I found appealing also frustrated me.

Where were the lists of allowed and forbidden foods? How was I supposed to know what to eat if there were no daily menus to follow? In my current way of thinking, I thought intermittent fasting seemed too extreme, too outside the mainstream and probably too good to be true.

Like most people, I grew up believing that breakfast is the most important meal of the day. It never occurred to me that the word breakfast had any relationship to the phrase break-the-fast. Everybody "knew" that breakfast meant to eat something within minutes of waking up or you would most definitely go into starvation mode and devour your own muscle and quite possibly die.

I also grew up in the era of Saturday morning cartoons, so I was pretty convinced that the best breakfasts involved bright colors, cool shapes and, of course, marshmallows. When I lost the weight on a vegetarian diet, I still believed that a traditional breakfast was important to get my metabolism going for the day, or I would lose energy like a wind-up toy by mid-morning. Even my foray into Paleo style eating was predicated on the importance of an early breakfast for the same reasons. What I was eating for breakfast changed a lot over the years, but I never really wavered from the practice of consuming food within an hour or so of waking up. But here was Dr. Herring suggesting not only was it ok to skip breakfast, but you could also skip lunch, too, and be healthier for it. It seemed radical to me, but I decided to try it.

I lasted one day. Seriously. When my eating window opened at 2:00 pm, I began eating and didn't stop until I went to bed. After years of jumping on restrictive dietary bandwagons, I couldn't deal with the concept of eating what I wanted, and I certainly was not willing to hear Dr. Herring's gentle assurances about compensatory overeating at the beginning of an IF lifestyle. At that time, I wanted clear, rigid rules, and I was stuck in the pattern of throwing everything away with a sense of failure with any perceived setback. I call it the "one grape too many" phenomenon. If you don't get it perfectly right, then scrap it for a new and better diet tomorrow.

For me that "better diet" was the low carb high-fat diet that I ultimately used to lose 120 pounds. Ironically, intermittent fasting was a hot topic in that world. Many of the Paleo writers and YouTube vloggers that I followed also talked about IF as a tool for weight loss and other health benefits. The two philosophies are complementary. Paleo is based on the premise that humans evolved to eat natural, unprocessed food in far less rigid patterns than the Standard American diet.

After all, cavemen didn't have Lucky Charms or refrigerators, so they spend much of their day hunting and gathering, consuming the bulk of their daily calories at the end of the day when they finally found a field of berries or took down a wooly mammoth. Intermittent fasting replicates that pattern in the modern world. As I became more and more invested in the Paleo way of eating, my flirtation with IF continued, but I didn't feel motivated to try it since it appeared that what I was doing was working just fine.

As the summer of 2017 approached, Kim and I continued to gain weight. We were both desperate to get back on our plans before we gained any more, but we were finding it increasingly difficult to settle back into the patterns that seemed to work for us in the past. Kim began looking for a better way. In another ironic twist, she became interested in intermittent fasting herself.

IF has some significant common ground with the Carbohydrate Addict's diet that had helped Kim lose 50 pounds. She was already eating low carb during the day and restricting her consumption of carbs to a one-hour dinner in the evening. It seemed like a reasonable leap to jump to a full IF protocol. While searching Pinterest for intermittent fasting for women, Kim saw an image for the cover of Gin Stephens' *Delay Don't Deny*. The title alone was enough to convince her to buy the book on Amazon.

For Kim, Gin's book was a revelation. Although inspired by Dr. Herring's work, Gin presents IF in an especially relatable way. She tried all the diets and bought all the products and books, but it wasn't until she began eating within a restricted eating window that she found easy, sustainable weight loss. More importantly, Gin made it clear that fat loss has far more to do with when we eat than the specifics of what we eat. She eats a wide variety of foods, but she doesn't eliminate any particular food group.

This resonated strongly for Kim whose main objection to my way of eating was the ban on most carbs. Although I had been reading about IF for years, I had a hard time embracing Gin's approach. I was scared of carbs, especially the really delicious ones like bread, pasta, and potatoes. I didn't want to gain more weight, and I was even more concerned about my blood sugar readings.

Despite my misgivings, the idea of being to able to eat more normally was appealing to me. I was tentative but also excited at the idea that Kim and I could actually eat the same meals and fully support each other's health-related goals for the first time in our marriage. Kim went all in, and I decided to follow her lead and jump in with both feet shortly after.

Kim: Finding Freedom

Ryan is absolutely spot-on that my discovery of Gin's book was "a revelation." It is a moment I will look back on forever as the turning point in my physical, mental and emotional life. Here is exactly how it happened. One evening as Emma's graduation loomed and I agonized about my out-of-control eating, I began searching Pinterest for weight loss ideas for women and stumbled back onto two critical words: Intermittent Fasting.

I remembered the concept from Ryan's reading of Dr. Herring's *Fast-5 Diet* book years earlier. Going deeper into that search, which included mostly infographics on how to time an eating window or bulleted lists of the health benefits of IF, I saw the picture of the cover of a book I had never heard of; I would later find out the book had been in publication a mere six months at that moment in time.

The book was called *Delay, Don't Deny: Living an Intermittent Fasting Lifestyle* by Gin Stephens. The symmetry and design of the cover, alternating empty plates with images of sumptuous food, appealed to me. The idea of delaying the foods I wanted to eat instead of giving them up fascinated me; that had always been the most appealing part of the Carb Addict's plan. I had a strong, unexplainable instinct that something significant had just happened to me. I look back on the moment I decided to do more than skim past the pin, the moment I typed "Delay, Don't Deny" into the Google search bar, as one of pure kismet.

Everything I read gave me a sense that the plan would work for my particular food-related challenges. I ordered a copy of the book on Amazon.com. I immediately joined Gin's Facebook group that accompanies the book, which at that point (May 2017) had about 4000 members. At the time of this writing, it has swelled to over 50,000 members. I started devouring every post in the group, learning all I could from other people who were already living this lifestyle. It quickly became apparent that my habit of drinking several cups of cream-filled coffee throughout the morning and afternoon was not congruent with a "clean fasting" protocol as Gin outlines it in the book. I knew I had to make the switch to black coffee if I were going to give myself any hope of success on this plan. I decided I would start the next morning.

No weaning, no tapering, my entire plan was this: pour a steaming cup of black coffee and drink it. I felt afraid. It now seems silly to be fearful of a cup of a simple beverage people drink all over the world, but at that point, I had a distinct inability to tolerate discomfort in the form of eating foods I did not like, resisting temptations or feeling hungry. These are all skills that fasting was soon to teach me, but in the moment, I was filled with dread.

I poured the coffee and stared at it like it was a cup of hot gasoline. I lifted the cup and smelled it, put it back down, then raised it to my lips and took a tiny sip that elicited a huge full-body shudder. It tasted awful to me. I didn't drink coffee at all until I was almost 30, and I had started with tons of cream and sugar, eventually ditching the sugar with the earliest rounds of Carb Addicts. But I had never in my life consumed a single sip of black coffee, and it was as bad as I'd thought it would be.

I choked down that cup of coffee. It was lukewarm by the time I was done, but the next day I did it again. Within a few days, as we got into June, I started doing black coffee on ice. Drinking it very cold through a straw muted the intensity of the flavor and I was tolerating it without grimacing. I carried a big Mason jar with a converted lid full of coffee to work every morning.

In addition to my new black coffee routine, I took what had been my (supposed) salad for lunch and whatever I wanted for dinner routine down to a late afternoon snack and whatever I wanted for dinner. After more than a year of mediocre cafeteria salads or "failing" by getting a sandwich, it was a relief not to eat lunch at all. Was I hungry? I guess so, but I was pretty used to doing most of my eating late in the day. The focus moved onto breaking my fast with a late afternoon snack, a process that evolved quite a bit in those first few weeks.

I tell the story of how at first, I broke my fast each afternoon with things like the coffee with cream that I'd delayed from the morning along with sweets like a muffin or cookie. I recall baking banana chocolate chip cookies for a potluck early in my fasting process and leaving two at home, then breaking my fast the next day by eating them smeared with a thick layer of peanut butter. It was really liberating to just eat things that I liked and feel I was sticking to a weight loss plan.

The only way I can answer questions like, "How quickly did you know this was going to work for you?", is that I knew right away. Within the first few days, my energy level soared. I felt so much more energetic and clear-headed through the morning hours than I had drinking coffee with cream. This was my first indication that the clean fast Gin promotes really did have significance. I can now see that by not stimulating insulin secretion with so much cream, I was able to go more quickly into a fat-burning state, which led me to feel fantastic. This is the reason I continue to emphasize the importance of clean fasting to anyone who learns about IF from me. It matters.

Working as a medical scribe for a surgeon who sees 16-18 patients in a clinic day is a job that requires mental focus and long hours on my feet. I quickly saw that this lifestyle was going to be of particular benefit to me at work. I think my coworkers wondered if I was going crazy, as my already positive attitude, something I'd been working on deliberately since my grandmother's death, seemed to border on euphoria at times. Physically, I have never felt as good as I did in those first three months of IF. I felt energized, almost electrified. I shared with my team that I was on a new eating plan but did not go into detail at that point.

Another sign that fasting was working for me was the shutting down of my constant craving for sugar. To my complete surprise, though the plan said I could break my fast with whatever food I wanted, I started to desire different foods. I started to crave roasted nuts, specifically cashews, and pistachios. I wanted cheeses like Havarti or cheddar, dips like hummus or guacamole, or even fresh avocado just sliced and salted. I found I did not want a muffin or cookie even when one was nearby. It sounded "too sweet" - a previously unheard-of concept. And those dinners I'd been eating through these years of trying to follow Carb Addict's Diet were changing too, becoming a little heavier on vegetables, a little lighter on pasta and bread.

I still had my nightly dessert but found I was fine with a couple squares of dark chocolate, not a stack of Oreos. I found myself opting for lighter, fruit-based desserts instead of the double fudge frenzy deluxe. The super sweet things I'd always loved simply didn't taste good anymore. I couldn't even fathom eating a big plate of Eggo waffles with syrup and chocolate chips before bed. Eating late in the evening was not a temptation or a desire. I felt full and satisfied from the time I closed my eating window.

My body started to change immediately, though I can't give numbers in pounds. I have never been someone to get on the scale very often. During the years of my peak weight gain, I never weighed myself at all, which is why it's difficult to say what my true all-time peak weight was. I don't have detailed statistics about how much weight came off in what amount of time. I'm sure that I started that summer of 2017 in a tight size 14W/16W and I was in size 10 by fall. It was the summer of my biggest body transformation ever. I made my way through a few weeks of being a size 12 by wearing old clothes from the back of the closet supplemented with a few Goodwill finds, but the itch to shop was getting strong.

The women reading this may relate to my obsession with sizes as much or more than the scale. I'd spent years - well over a decade - fantasizing about the elusive size 12, and here it was. I'm sure that somewhere along the way, the word "never" had come out of my mouth in regard to the possibility of wearing a size 10 again. I had been a size 10 in high school and at this point in my fasting journey, I figured I'd achieved the peak of my success. My results had truly exceeded the stuff of my dreams. Even though people urged me not to, I rushed out and bought a myriad of brand-new clothing items in size 10. It felt like I had arrived at the body I'd been dreaming of.

Throughout that summer and fall, Gin's Facebook group played such an important role in my daily life. I made posts to the group several times a week, and I read and commented on a daily basis. The 24-hour, 7-day-a-week nature made it as valuable, or more so, than a weekly face-to-face group. As my weight loss results became more dramatic, I started to post before-and-after photographs, often putting my current photo alongside a picture of me from the heaviest days around 2013-2014. People's reactions to these pictures were also beyond my wildest dreams - hundreds of comments calling me gorgeous, stunning and amazing.

I started to feel like a known commodity in the best possible way. New group members would ask questions about my journey, and others would chime in who had followed my story well enough to know how long I had been fasting, what kind of window I ate in, whether I did or didn't eat carbs or count calories. People referred to me as a rock star, as the "IF poster girl", and for someone who had just struggled through decades of self-doubt and poor self-image, it was a total thrill.

Because I was such a visible presence in the community, and because she has a huge heart for encouraging others, Gin herself took a personal interest in me. We became personal Facebook friends and corresponded regularly via private messaging. She encouraged me to believe that my body would continue to change if I stayed committed to the lifestyle.

I continued clean fasting and my body continued to change. Pictures through those months show subtle but steady changes to the contours of my face. My cheekbones and jawline came out in a way I'd never seen. My collarbones and ribcage became prominent. The roll of back fat along the bra line, present since my early 20s, melted completely away. It is important for me to clarify - I did not get skinny, nor am I skinny as I sit typing this. My body displays an amazing ability to build lean muscle and preserve just enough fat that I look healthy and well-nourished. Fear of being "too thin" is a self-protective thing very fat women endorse, and I said it myself, but I don't believe anyone would look at my body and say I am too thin.

As we reached December 2017, I seemed to practically skip size 8 and went right into size 6 jeans. This was a HUGE milestone that I crowed about in the group, and people were so supportive. I again thought that the changes to my body had finished, but Gin encouraged me to keep my mind open. When she made a post about having a couple pair of size 4 jeans from Loft that were too big for her, I joked that I wished she would send them to me because it would motivate me to keep going. She did.

It is hard for me to describe the feeling of receiving that package with the pairs of size 4 jeans inside. I felt overwhelmed by gratitude - for my health, for the strength I had found, for my new life, and for the friendship of this wonderful stranger who, through her belief in me, had helped me to believe in myself. I opened the package and stared at the jeans, feeling a bit of the fear that I felt when I poured that first cup of black coffee. I decided I could not try them on yet, having just gotten into my first size 6's, and I placed them in a safe spot and continued to do what I'd been doing for nine months - clean fasting every day and feasting every evening.

Several days later, the suspense began to get to me and I decided: I am going to try on Gin's jeans (this is what I still call them to this day). I wiggled into them, managed to get the zipper pulled to the top, and said to Ryan, "how do they look?", to which he responded with another question, "Can you breathe?" I had just enough oxygen to say not really, so I went to take them off, but the fact that they'd been on my body even briefly was exciting proof of progress.

Of course, I had to document the moment with a photograph and a picture to the group, which elicited a ton of supportive comments. It made me feel special that I was selected; obviously, Gin could not send her jeans to everyone, but I wanted those new to the group to understand just how personally invested she is in the success of the people who read her book and commit to her plan.

By late February and March of 2018, I was starting to move into a pre-maintenance of sorts, which had nothing to do with scale and everything to do with a sense of mastery where I had honed my proper eating window, the ideal types and amounts of food, and the incorporation of exercise to utilize my newfound high energy. I found myself taking longer, more frequent walks, and even taking it up to a sprint. I thought of all the dreaded running I'd been forced to do in PE, and as my feet pounded the pavement, I felt myself releasing the old narrative about the weak little girl who wasn't as worthy as the others.

Emma was living on campus in her first year of University, so the empty nest was closer than ever, yet life was just amazing. I felt totally in balance, and right around that time, Gin began to talk about rolling out Delay, Don't Deny support groups. Of course, I immediately considered getting involved. I had drawn so much benefit from being part of an online group and was intrigued by the idea of getting together face to face with like-minded fasting folks. Here was a chance to take another big step outside my comfort zone and I embraced it.

In preparation, I started my own Facebook group, which I titled Fasting, Feasting, FREEDOM: Intermittent Fasting Support with Kim. Within a few weeks, the group had grown to 100 members, most of whom were local to me, many of them folks I knew "in real life." It was great fun to come into my group and post tidbits of inspiration and share photos of the food I'd consumed within my daily window. I started to hear from a handful of those folks that IF was quickly clicking for them, and they were experiencing the same powerful effects I had months earlier. I was happy for them and it motivated me to share my story even more widely.

Around this time, I became rather restless at work. I felt I needed to talk, express myself, move more in the world. My scribe job is a quiet one, literally located in the background of the scene, and I was welling up with physical energy and emotional passion. I began to think about how I could start an entrepreneurial "side hustle". I found myself up early on Saturdays and Sundays, sitting in Starbucks with my cup of black Pike's Place blend and a bottle of San Pellegrino, ideas running through my mind. I began joining lots of online freelancing communities and making connections with like-minded women.

Dr. Starks and I contemplated a startup business to recruit and train scribes for other physicians because we knew the need was great, but after months of research, the work involved in scaling was too huge for the two of us. It still lit a fire under me to have tried something like that. Through April and May, I attended local networking events and entrepreneurial meetups, going out often for drinks, dinner and other social gatherings. Meeting people felt easy and comfortable. I surprised myself by saying yes to opportunities when in the past, I quickly said no.

I felt confident getting dressed in lots of cute new clothes for these occasions. I was buying blouses in size small and even extra-small, a size I used to scoff at when shopping a few years earlier. There is one particular size small top that I bought for Emma her freshman year of high school; I now call it the "triumph blouse." Even though I didn't pay much attention to her clothes, I had stared longingly at this one item, believing that even if I lost some weight, I'd never lose enough to fit into it.

That spring, Emma was living in her dorm room and the blouse was in her closet at our house. Her style preferences had changed as rapidly as my weight, and the special blouse was forgotten until I pulled it out and tried it on one day. It fit, and for a while, I wore it frequently just on principle.

I started buying similar floral tops to the triumph blouse along with skinny jeans and ballet flats as a signature look, a stark contrast to my previous fat "uniform" of baggy jeans, XXL tank tops and oversized cardigans I could wrap around to hide my midsection. I started buying and wearing dresses, just for fun. I started to notice I had my hand on my hip in every photograph, where in the past, I always crossed my arms across the front of me, placed my purse in front of me, or grabbed the nearest small child to stand behind. My whole self-image had transformed.

I realized that I was getting the biggest response from people in Gin's group when I posted photos taken together with Ryan. It was like our combined weight loss had an exponentially more dramatic effect than either of us separately. Ryan was getting more involved in the larger IF community on the internet and had joined several groups that I was not in. He agreed to be an administrator for my group with me, so I changed the name to Fasting, Feasting, FREEDOM with Kim and Ryan.

As the months have gone on and the group has steadily grown to its current 2000 members, I have heard from particular individuals that my story, my inspiration and encouragement, made a difference in their progress. It showed me that I have an opportunity through my efforts to "be someone's Gin." It is difficult to explain how meaningful this feels to me. Going all the way back to childhood, I felt drawn toward teaching, counseling and encouraging others. Now, because of a decision initially motivated by food and weight, I am finding my own voice to spread a message of hope to those who feel stuck in patterns that keep them obese. It brings me genuine joy.

As this chapter has been quite rosy, I should address the question of whether or not there were any parts of the journey that were especially challenging or constituted a struggle. I've presented a fairly pretty picture of what it was like to start fasting, settle quickly into a groove, and then just have my weight drop and my body transform like magic. It may not have been quite that simple, but that really is the basic story. It's a classic case of when it's right, it's right, and just like a single person who struggles through dating disappointments and failed relationships, when that person finally meets The One, past frustrations fade into the background. I feel like intermittent fasting is the lifestyle I was meant to live, and while I don't waste energy wishing I had found it sooner, I believe it is the way I'll eat for the rest of my life.

One challenging aspect of my transformation has been shedding my former identity as an obese woman. Only people who have been really heavy will relate to this. This is not the same thing as the typical American woman who says she's fat, wants to lose 10 or 15 pounds because she's unhappy with how she looks in a swimsuit. This is about having taken on a new identity as the "fat mom" or the "fat friend" in a given group. I was always the heaviest mother when my children were in school. Does it matter? Maybe not, but it had become part of the way I saw myself in the world.

Over the course of less than a year, I went from often being the largest woman in a given group to being the smallest. It is still taking time for my head to catch up. I spent a lot of time looking in mirrors and taking pictures of myself. The selfies served a dual purpose: I could post them to encourage and inspire others in the Facebook groups, but also gaze at them myself, trying to internalize this identity as a normal weight person, a person who meets new acquaintances who have no idea of my past weight problem unless I choose to share it.

There is a bit of a sense of having betrayed other women who are still heavy, those who had been my comrades, so to speak. I was somewhere, and a lady made a joke to the effect of, "I'm a fat girl. We don't do stairs if we can help it." I instinctively looked up with the expectation that she'd meet my eye and we'd share that knowing laugh of two people with a shared reality. I realized she was not even looking in my direction. We'd met recently, and she had no idea I used to be 100 pounds overweight. It was such a mixed emotion to realize she perceived me as a thin person. It felt like I'd lost a tribe of sorts.

The same is true to this moment when I hear about the body positive movement, which is a social media campaign through which women of all sizes (but overwhelmingly, larger women) are embracing their size and shape and proclaiming their beauty. I ask myself if I am wrong to feel I look better/healthier or consider myself more attractive now. I ponder whether I am just conforming to narrow standards of ideal female beauty. Physically, I feel freer than I ever have, and I'm not sorry to admit this: I am happy the weight is gone.

Probably the hardest part of this whole process are the people who've been envious or critical. Do you know the expression,

"Watch those people who don't clap when you win?" Well, that phenomenon is real. And though I have been envious of other people's weight loss success in the past (including Ryan's), it still stung when I had people in my real life who, instead of being thrilled for me, ignored my results or made smug comments about me starving myself. It felt invalidating to work so hard on something and not have that effort acknowledged. However, I did not let this deter or discourage me for long.

I think fasting has true power through the fact that it is such a non-conforming social behavior. When you begin to embrace fasting as a lifestyle, it helps you detach from the need for other people's approval. Stating you are not going to eat during the day is a mundane and yet radical decision to make. Thus, when I was met with other people's jealousy or negativity, I was able to shake it off quickly and reaffirm that I was on this journey for myself and my health.

For me as a formerly frightened, insecure little girl, this has been the greatest triumph of the entire process. I have learned to live with radical self-acceptance and acknowledgment of my fundamental worth. At this stage in my life, self-care is my highest goal, and daily fasting is the centerpiece of my regimen.

My persona now is one of boundless energy and positivity for life and all the (non-food) pleasures it has to offer. I was noted to have been a non-excitable child, serious and solemn, but I'm now thought of as someone genuinely excited about most everything. My Instagram account is @hookedonenthusiasm because that is how I feel most of the time. I love the experience of being alive. The world and the people in it are exquisitely beautiful to me, at least most of the time. I appreciate all the unique qualities that come together to create my unique self.

I do believe in God and I pray daily, sometimes hourly. I also believe in New Age-y concepts like vibes, energy, and the law of attraction. I broadly refer to that stuff as 'woo woo' and I love it. Never enough woo for me these days. I live by the principles of radical self-acceptance and I'm overwhelmed by gratitude for all the blessings I've been given in my life.

As we close the part of this book about me as an individual, I invite you to picture that little girl I opened with, me. I was on the sidelines at field day, and I wanted nothing more than to fade into the backdrop. Everyone else was laughing and having fun, but I was missing out.

Contrast that with a recent Saturday night when I danced in a nightclub for four hours straight. That evening, like every day now, I felt strong, energetic, and comfortable in every inch of my skin. Clad in jeans and a tight-fitting top in the center of the dance floor, I was probably attracting attention, but it didn't matter. I'm no longer self-conscious or uneasy. I have no need for approval from others about my appearance or any of my qualities. Finally, I know what was true all along, that I am beautiful, and I am free.

Ryan: Bringing it all Together

My first few weeks of intermittent fasting can be described as tentative at best. I believed that IF could be effective, but I had been viewing it through the lens of low carb for years. My most recent weight loss was accomplished through low carb eating, and I was reluctant to give that up for multiple reasons. I had deeply internalized the idea that carbs were the enemy, and my good blood sugar control was tied directly to that diet. I didn't want to go backward with my health. I was now in my 40's, and I knew that I would not have unlimited chances to turn things around.

I'm not sure why I was so dubious about Gin's way of eating since I ate a lot of carbs when I lost weight on a vegetarian diet, and my blood sugar numbers were great. It was a mindset issue. I guess on some level I felt that if I abandoned Paleo/low carb, it would be an admission of defeat.

I was invested in Paleo, but I was more invested in trying something that would allow Kim and me to finally share a way of eating. I committed to a clean fast of nineteen hours and an eating window of five hours, usually 2-7pm. Kim was eager to try Plated, a meal delivery service that sends ingredients and recipes to your home. She wanted to simplify meal planning and was frankly tired of trying to figure out how to prepare food that would satisfy different preferences.

I was skeptical of the home delivery meals because many of the meals contained carbs like potatoes or rice, and I had been rejecting those foods for some time. I decided to compromise. I would eat Paleo foods in my eating window......except for dinner when I would eat the Plated meals. In an ironic twist, I was setting up a Carbohydrate Addict's Diet protocol, the very diet Kim was eager to move on from.

I started my first fast in June 2017, shortly after finishing a school year. As a teacher, I was accustomed to having summers off, and eating had been a major way of passing the time. In my earlier, unhealthy years, the summer weeks were basically a non-stop binge with lots of empty promises to myself that I would get it together, start a new diet and take weight off before I had to buy new school clothes. Most of those summers ended with frustration, self-loathing and the next waist size up from the previous June.

Even in my healthy summers, when I was eating vegetarian or later after Paleo, I used food as a way to structure my day and manage my emotions. One of the things that I professed to love about being a vegetarian was my ability to eat every few hours. I held that up as a badge of honor, proof that my metabolism was firing on all cylinders and I was in a perpetual fat-burning state. Looking back on it now, I realize that I was constantly hungry, constantly coming down from excessive carbs and constantly on the edge of a major dietary blowout.

Paleo summers were not much different, though the food choices were. Kim and I would often bargain with each other to white knuckle it to 11:00 am, the earliest socially acceptable time to eat lunch, when we would eat a big salad with protein. For me, this was on the heels of a bacon and eggs breakfast at 7:00 am and a snack of nuts and cheese at 9:00 am. Suddenly, I was facing the prospect of a day without food until 2:00 pm, and I was a little daunted.

Overall the initial fasts were much easier than I expected them to be. I did not feel particularly hungry, and I definitely did not get faint or feel weak. I tried to keep busy with household projects, long walks with my dogs, and shamelessly excessive Netflix binges. Physically it was pretty easy, but psychologically it was more difficult.

Typically, I would be eyeing the clock by noon and would have a hanging-on-by-my-fingertips sensation for that final couple of hours. I steeled my resolve, believing that it would get better over time. I opened my window every day with what I called "Paleo cereal", basically a bowl full of chia seeds, nuts, berries, and peanut butter with milk or cream poured over the top. Kim always thought this was a weird combination, but I love it, and it was a breakfast staple during my low-carb weight loss.

Once I started eating, I sometimes found it difficult to stop. I might eat more food than I originally planned, or I might desperately want to, but actively resist. It was uncomfortable and familiar behavior, but I remembered Dr. Herring's warnings about compensatory overeating. This was normal, and I trusted that my appetite would moderate in time.

Dinners were completely new and much more satisfying experience. For the first time, Kim and I were not only eating the same food at the same time, but we were also spending more time cooking together. There was no need for leftovers since I was not packing lunches for the next day. I soon discovered that I was completely satisfied after dinner and no longer felt a strong desire to eat something before bed.

Although I initially vowed to include carbs like potatoes and rice in my dinner meal only, I soon started introducing other foods that I had been denying myself for a long time. I started adding whole grain crackers or tortilla chips with hummus to break my fasts. We started eating desserts after dinner every night. Sometimes the desserts were glorified breakfast foods like yogurt with berries, but sometimes it was chocolate or more sugary treats like Gelato or cookies.

I was conflicted about eating these kinds of foods. On the one hand, I was thrilled and realized that I missed eating a wider range of foods. It felt so normal and real and good to scoop up some hummus with a chip instead of chasing it around the plate with a piece of cheese. On the other hand, I experienced a bit of "Paleo guilt". I had spent a long time eating in a restricted manner that I loudly touted as the way to sustainable weight loss. I had spent countless hours watching videos and reading blogs and telling anyone that would listen that I owed my health to high fat low carb eating.

Now I was doing something else that would likely be seen as radical by all the people who already thought eating a bowl of spaghetti sauce without the spaghetti was a little nutty. I decided to push through those nagging doubts and let the results speak for themselves.

It wasn't long, maybe two weeks, when I realized that fasting was having some quick and dramatic results. I was feeling great during the fast and had plenty of energy to go on long hikes or do prolonged chores, like painting the living room without food breaks. I had occasional hunger pangs, but they passed within minutes. Unlike previous weight loss efforts, I learned to truly recognize the difference between physical hunger and an emotional desire to eat. Both were easier to ignore than I had ever experienced before. The pounds that I regained in my last few months of Paleo started coming off steadily, and I didn't feel like I was depriving myself or working out excessively to achieve it.

By the time I was preparing to go back to work in the fall, I was almost back to my goal weight. I was excited about the ways fasting would change my school day routines, but also a little nervous about what I was going to tell people about what I was doing. I knew that something was different about this round of weight loss. It felt more permanent and normal to me, but I worried that others would find it strange or inwardly judge me for jumping on another dietary bandwagon.

I focused on the practical ways that fasting would make my day easier. I didn't have to pack a lunch or think about the time crunch created by standing in a line for the microwave. I could use my lunch break to make a quick photocopy, fire off some emails or just socialize with my colleagues. I thought that I could fly under the radar with my new way of eating for a while, but it attracted attention on the second day.

A fellow English teacher noticed that I wasn't eating, assumed that I had forgotten my lunch, and offered to share her food with me. I wasn't ready to explain IF to anyone at that point, so I just said, "I'm not eating lunch these days. I'm doing a thing." That was all it took for people to accept that I didn't eat at the same time as anyone else. Nobody asked any questions or mentioned it in any way until more dramatic results became increasingly obvious.

Although I reached my goal weight quickly, my body continued to change in ways that it never had with any other diet plan. In fact, IF is the first way of eating I've ever done in which weight and pounds have become secondary to these other kinds of changes. I began to notice that my face was getting more angular and defined. I had a jawline for the first time. My collar bones and the muscles in my legs and arms became more prominent. My biggest problem area, my stomach, was beginning to tighten up, and I was beginning to see the shadow of ab muscles under the loose skin and stubborn belly fat that I had never been able to conquer.

As a fat man and a formerly fat man, I had come to accept that I would always have to pull up my pants continuously because my belt landed below my gut. One day as I was walking down the hallway at school, I realized that my pants were staying put. I was bowled over to realize that my belt was at my natural waistline, something that probably hadn't happened since I was eight years old!

As I noticed these changes in my body, I was more motivated than ever to make more changes to maximize my physical fitness. I figured that if my stomach could actually tone up, then I might be capable of even more. I had been fascinated by yoga for several years, but I had never actually tried to do it. I subscribed to a YouTube channel called *ManFlowYoga*, which focuses on yoga for muscle building and overall fitness. I had watched countless videos and made playlists of the workouts that I thought I might be physically capable of, but I had never tried to do it. Intermittent fasting gave me the confidence to stand up, roll out the mat, and just do it. My first year of fasting coincided with my first year of yoga practice. It's the first formal method of exercise that I have loved and maintained for more than a few weeks.

For me, the practice of fasting and the practice of yoga have been perfectly complementary. Both are gentle and functional ways of improving overall health and wellness. Both promote muscle activation and growth. Both are integral to making changes to my body that I didn't think I would ever see. Losing and regaining 120 pounds twice in my life has created some scars that may never completely go away, but I now know that I am capable of so much more than I believed for so long.

Eventually, people around me began to respond to these changes and ask me about what I was doing. Most people would say something like, "Oh, you're losing so much weight. How much have you lost?" Most people didn't believe me when I said that the scale hadn't moved in months. We're so conditioned to measure our successes in pounds, but the body is capable of improving in ways that defy this arbitrary number.

I think people were noticing that my posture was improving, my shoulders were slightly broader, my natural jawline was becoming visible, and I was starting to look younger. I like to think that intermittent fasting restores the body to factory settings, that it's molding me to closer to what I was meant to be if I had never gained all that weight in the first place.

Although many of the changes I've experienced since starting IF have been physical, I have changed on the inside as well. I'm reserved by nature, but I am more confident and comfortable in my skin now. I'm a better teacher because I enjoy being "on stage" in front of my students much more, and I am more willing and able to be myself with them.

I think I'm a better husband, too, because Kim and I are sharing our lives in a much bigger way now. Kim's passion for IF inspired me to try it as well, and our mutual passion for this lifestyle gives our marriage a larger and fulfilling purpose. We're better partners now, and people can see that we truly enjoy each other. I like to think that other people around us are inspired by the changes they see in us to make positive changes in their lives as well.

One of the greatest changes for which I am very grateful is that I am feeling a shift in my identity as a healthy and fit man. I no longer feel like I am on a diet, struggling to maintain a bunch of difficult if not impossible rules. I eat like a "real person". More importantly, fasting has transformed my overall relationship with food. Without food as a constant way to push down emotions, I am learning to actually feel them and deal with them productively.

This is a forever change. I'm a work in progress for sure. I still occasionally battle feelings of depression and anxiety, but for the first time in my life, I am confident that things are just going to get better from here.

IF: This is What We Do

One of the most common questions Kim and I receive from people who are interested in our story is, "What exactly do you eat?" Every diet book I ever purchased, and there are many, was an attempt to answer that question for myself. I was looking for someone to take all the guesswork out of the process. I wanted so desperately to get it right, and I thought a list or set of rules could do that for me.

When I was a teenager and already feeling angst about my weight, my mother had a copy of the Overeaters Anonymous book. I don't recall her ever being a member of OA, so I suspect she bought that book in her own futile attempt to get the answer. I remember reading that book, looking for the list of forbidden foods, the set of rules that I could implement that would cure me of overeating. Anyone familiar with Overeaters Anonymous recognizes that I was barking up the wrong tree. I was completely unable to see the value in that book, which is more about healing the addiction than putting a band-aid on it. The search continued for many years.

The beauty and the frustration of intermittent fasting are in its simplicity. The "rules" are deceptively simple: clean fast for about 19 hours then eat your daily nutrition in approximately 5 hours. How one chooses to eat in the eating window is really up to the individual. IF is a tool that can be equally beneficial to the vegan or the carnivore. Some people eat low carb in the window, and some people eat lots of carbs. Dr. Herring refers to the "experiment of one", which is a simple way of saying that everyone has to figure out what they like to eat and what works best for their body.

Does this mean you can fast for 19 hours then eat beefaroni and jelly beans for 5 straight hours? Sure, you can. It's a free country. Will you see the results you want if you eat a junk diet? Probably not. Intermittent fasting works best with a combination of common sense and flexibility, but that does not look the same for everyone.

Kim and I have figured out what works for us. We've had amazing results while eating a wide range of foods in our window. We eat a LOT of food, including fat and carbs, probably the scariest and most controversial of the macros. Sometimes people will comment, mostly in jest, that we are "going to fade away" or we are "half the people we used to be". I think these light-hearted comments mask a real fear that the only way to lose weight is to be miserable and deprived, to starve your body into submission.

We have the best relationship with food that we've ever had. We love to eat, and we still eat not only for nourishment but for entertainment and celebration. The key difference is when we eat, and how that change has helped us manage our sugar addiction and binge-eating behaviors.

People are often surprised when we describe what and how we eat. This section of the book is not intended to be a list of forbidden and acceptable foods, nor is it a menu of what you should eat. It's simply an illustration of what works for us. It's our hope that it will be encouraging for others to see that it's possible, and easier than you might think, to refrain from eating for relatively long periods of time, and to be satisfied when you do eat, all without severe restriction or obsessive calorie counting. Intermittent fasting can do all that and more.

Kim and I start each day with a clean fast as recommended by Gin in *Delay Don't Deny*. This means we don't consume anything except water, black coffee or plain tea until we break the fast in the mid to late afternoon. Many people who are thinking about starting a fasting protocol worry - understandably - about these hours most of all. I've had friends, colleagues and family members say, "Oh, I could never go that long without eating! Don't you get hungry? I would get weak or dizzy if I try that!" We have been so conditioned to think that we need to eat often to avoid dire consequences that we ignore our common sense.

How can the human body be such a complex, intricate machine, yet break down its own muscle after a few hours without food? Our ability to have quick and convenient food sources is a relatively modern invention, but we have been on the planet for thousands of years. Surely we were not sickly and weak, barely surviving as a species, until Goldfish crackers came along to stave off extinction! You only need to visit your local department store to know that convenience foods and non-stop snacking is not the answer to robust health and fitness.

Many new fasters do feel hungry, slightly weak or dizzy, or extremely preoccupied with food at the beginning of the process as the body adjusts to not receiving an influx of calories steadily throughout the day. Have you ever tried to convince a food-motivated beagle to reduce his daily biscuit ration from three biscuits to one? He will not go down without a fight. The human body will typically resist as well, but after it learns that food is not coming, it will adapt to its new reality and begin burning stored fat for fuel.

Some of these initial feelings are physical and can be powered through. Remember that you will be feasting later and can have your fill. Some of the feelings are purely psychological. You may be bored or anxious and suddenly your primary coping mechanism is gone. Kim and I had to find other ways to use our time and mental energy, and once we did, daily fasts became easier. In any event, hunger is not an emergency. You will find that waves of hunger may come and go throughout the day. When you become more comfortable with the process, the passing pangs are a reassuring sign that your body is burning fat.

Kim and I were already in very different places on meals when we decided to start fasting. Kim had been drinking multiple cups of coffee with cream throughout the day. I drank my coffee black, but I was also eating breakfast early in my day, often by 5:00 am. My first meal of the day was generally big and calorically dense, things like bacon and eggs, or yogurt with peanut butter and berries. Both of us had to sacrifice something we enjoyed having, but the common denominator for us was the coffee.

Once Kim learned to drink her coffee black, we were able to make our love of coffee a shared experience and a centerpiece of our fast. We experiment with different brands and roasts. Instead of going out to eat, we hang out in different coffee shops and cafes, sipping hot or iced black coffee, talking and people watching. Sometimes people who don't like coffee at all will ask in a slightly wary tone if coffee is mandatory for intermittent fasting. The answer is a resounding no! If you don't like coffee, don't drink it. It is important to develop positive rituals to replace the ones that have disappeared, so your new lifestyle doesn't feel like misery and deprivation over the long haul.

Kim and I extended our fasts until 2:00 - 3:00 pm even at the beginning, so we also had to contend with the afternoon hours that would typically kick off with some kind of lunch. Just like with breakfast, it's mostly a mindset issue, a decision to delay eating and developing new ways to spend the time. Energy levels are often very high during the fasted state, so it's an ideal time for physical activity. I started doing yoga around the time I began fasting. I typically do 15-30 minute workouts, 4-5 times per week. I think yoga is awesome because it's low impact but builds muscle and improves flexibility. Kim and I walk a lot, together and separately. We both have wristband trackers and use them to aim for a daily 10,000 step goal. Kim often goes for a short walk on her lunch break at work. It's a good way to recharge for the second half of the day rather than eating a meal in the middle of the day that leaves you tired and bloated.

After a long period of time without food, it's time to break the fast. As a general rule, we consider a 5-hour eating window to be our maximum, so we generally open the window in the ballpark of 2-4 pm, but that can vary from day to day. On weekends or vacation days, we tend to open at the same time and with the same foods, but when we are working, we do our own thing.

Although we feel free to open the window with whatever foods we want, we have discovered that we feel best when we eat with a combination of protein, fat and small amounts of carbs. Our most common go-to for breaking the fast is our "nibbly plate". We fill up two small appetizer plates with multigrain chips or crackers, generous scoops of hummus, 2-3 olives, a few slices of cheese and a small handful of nuts. We don't measure anything or worry about calorie counts. We eyeball it based on how hungry we feel, and how long it is likely to be until dinner. Kim often adds a glass of kombucha on the side. It's a fermented, slightly fizzy tea beverage that has multiple health benefits. It's one of the very rare foods that Kim likes, and I don't. She finds it to be energizing and tasty while I think it tastes like straight vinegar.

When breaking the fast alone, I tend to go back to my Paleo toolbox for a high fat, relatively low sugar snack. One of my favorite options is what I like to call a "busy bowl". I like so many little food items that sometimes I throw a bunch of things in a bowl and mix them all together. I typically start with Greek yogurt, plain or maybe vanilla, as a base. I stir in peanut butter and chia seeds, then top with mixed nuts, dried fruit, fresh berries, a few chocolate chips, whatever I'm in the mood to eat.

Kim finds these bowls to be a little too busy for her taste, so she goes more minimalist when she breaks the fast on her own. Her favorite snack is a Perfect Bar, protein bars based on organic nut butter and a powdered superfood blend She has described her love for these bars as an addiction and tends to eat one every day, either as her break-the-fast or as a dessert after dinner. Sometimes she opens with an iced coffee with cream or an espresso latte.

This is how we choose to break our fasts, but some people do not eat anything until dinner, a true One Meal a Day, or OMAD. Others eat different kinds or amounts of food that work for them. It's highly individual how a faster chooses to "open the window," but we select foods that make us feel good, that leave us temporarily satisfied but not overly full, so we can still enjoy our dinner. Usually, we wait between 1 and 3 hours after breaking the fast to prepare dinner, our one main meal of the day.

Our evening meal has become much more intentional since we began fasting. We are typically only eating one full meal per day, so we always want it to be something substantive and nutritious, but more importantly, delicious and fun to eat. As with most aspects of this journey, meal planning and prep has evolved a lot since our unhealthy eating days.

Kim's discovery of IF coincided with a peak in her frustration with budgeting for groceries and planning what to eat each day. It had always been a struggle to make a meal that everyone would eat. Even when the kids were elsewhere and we were cooking for two, we didn't eat the same foods for most of our marriage unless we were eating junk food. Both of us working towards wellness at the same time in a similar way was a brand-new experience. Kim started reading about meal delivery services like Plated and Home Chef, companies that send boxes of ingredients and recipes to make your own amazing meals at home.

In typical fashion, I was reluctant to embrace this change because I wasn't convinced that I could eat carbs and reach my health goals, and I was intimidated by the perceived complexity of the cooking techniques involved. Kim really sold the idea to me as a way to control our budget, our portions, our food waste, and as something fun to do as a couple.

We received our first meal deliveries in June of 2017, and they were an immediate hit with us. The meal preparation was definitely more complicated than we were accustomed to, but we were happy to realize that not only could we successfully produce the meals, but they actually looked like the picture on the front of the recipe card and tasted awesome. The meals used a lot of fresh vegetables and herbs and included simple sauces that really elevated the quality of the whole plate. We loved trying new things, like salmon poke bowls, roasted vegetables, and fish tacos.

These meals really set the standard for how we like to eat and heavily influenced how we make a meal on our own and how we eat in restaurants. We feel the best when we eat meals that are a combination of protein, carbs and fat, including salmon, chicken, pork, potatoes, rice, quinoa, all kinds of vegetables, creamy sauces with plenty of olive oil and butter. Sometimes we add salad or avocado to the meal if we feel it's a little too light.

We also eat some kind of dessert almost every night. Some nights we have golden milk, a turmeric-based hot beverage that is soothing and anti-inflammatory, with a few squares of dark chocolate. Other we might have a more traditional dessert, like a piece of cake or a couple of cookies if something special presents itself. Over time, we've developed better instincts about knowing when we are satisfied without being uncomfortably full. We've learned that a varied and interesting diet really fuels our fasts for the next day.

Kim and I never count calories, fat grams or carb grams. We don't write down what we eat in a food journal. We don't refuse to eat any particular kind of food as a rule that we must follow to consider our day a success. We work in an ongoing way to reject the diet mentality that sabotaged our efforts in the past. This flexibility is key to finding the sweet spot with intermittent fasting.

We typically choose to eat in a window of 3-4 hours from approximately 3:00-7:00 pm, but we change it up for special occasions or when life throws us a curveball. Last Christmas was an especially food-filled day for us. We were planning to go to Kim's father's house for a Christmas morning gathering, but a major snowstorm forced us to stay home. We ate a traditional breakfast that day and probably ate in an 8-hour window.

That's not our norm, but it worked that day. On my father's birthday last month, we broke the fast with coffee and a big piece of cake in the middle of the afternoon. Again, this is unusual for us, but we find fasting to be so forgiving that exceptions to the norm are not something to fear, or an excuse to throw in the towel.

Everyone needs to figure out what works best for themselves and that may not match conventional diet wisdom. We have found intermittent fasting to be the most effective way to shake off the chains of addictive overeating and just live with true freedom around food.

Our Marriage and Our Future

If you picked up this book knowing it had a happy ending, here it comes. This time in our marriage truly feels like we have been granted a fresh new start. People often reflect that we look younger than ever and we feel it. We got married at ages 30 and 31, but now at 45 and 46, it feels like we are back in honeymoon mode as we engage with life and each other much like we did in the early days, only better. No, we don't recommend that couples gain 200+ pounds and then lose it as a way to spice things up, but it is what has happened to us and we embrace the journey and its lessons. We have a deeper level of intimacy than we ever have, and it's a great time to behave like newlyweds since our nest is pretty much empty.

Looking back, Ryan and I own the fact that we used food as a way to celebrate every good day and push down negative feelings on bad days. There was nothing in our wedding vows about food, but perhaps there should have been. Food was easy when marriage was hard, and we used it to avoid addressing and working through our problems. Food became this thing that grew and metastasized and came between us. It was a barrier as we tried to connect with each other, and it was an obstacle between us and the rest of the world.

As food was relegated to its proper place in the background of life, we have been forced to find new ways to interact with each other and to spend time alone, a particularly slippery slope for people who have issues with food. However, we are in a calm and centered place where we are patient with ourselves and each other as we navigate new territory.

Our life now revolves around trying to do the things that will make us feel healthy and good. We plan and eat meals that we absolutely love, and with rare exception, our plates look identical. We can go off on a hike without packing any food, and we can leave for a day trip without the expense of buying breakfast or lunch out somewhere. We've always been homebodies and really do enjoy spending time close to home, so we try to appreciate the simple things in life. We're fortunate to live in close proximity to a waterfront park. We walk our dog there every day just to enjoy the sounds of the water, the wildflowers and the many birds that live near the river. Connecting to nature is an effective way to disconnect from stressors that trigger a desire to eat when we're really not hungry.

We spend a lot of quiet time on our screened-in porch as well. It's absolutely the best part of our house, and we love to spend summer afternoons out there, talking through our day and planning for the next one. It's a far cry from our previous pattern of eating until we were painfully stuffed then watching TV in silence until it was time to go to bed. We love to plan our meals ahead. We cook and try new foods on our date nights. Going to coffeehouses to people watch and try different roasts of black coffee is a favorite fasted thing to do.

Our happiest times are having Adam and Emma at the house to celebrate holidays or just have dinner with us. I'm so proud of the young adults they've become and the bond they have with one another. It's a whole new ballgame to have a life without them, since they were part of our relationship from the very beginning.

Even though Ryan and I love being together, we also enjoy individual pursuits. I love to shop and hunt for bargains with Emma and truly consider her my best friend. She's quite busy as a full-time University of Maine student, so I am working on developing a wide range of hobbies of my own. I like to go out with a group of friends to dance or sing karaoke. It used to make me anxious to spend time alone, but now I appreciate the chance to have the house to myself or take a long walk with just my thoughts. And of course, if you follow my online activities, you know I love social media, making tons of Instagram posts on my personal account, running our Facebook IF group and writing entries for the blog on our website.

Ryan would rather skip the drinks and dancing most of the time. He enjoys Marvel movies on the big screen, but they don't hold much interest for me, so he goes with his friend Jeremy to spare me the superheroes the way I spare him the karaoke. He likes many TV shows and documentaries that aren't my style. This summer he has rediscovered his love of all things Stephen King and has spent many lazy afternoons reading his most recent novel. I am impressed by Ryan's consistent yoga practice and amazed by the strength and flexibility he has gained. I see so much positive change in him, yet none of it surprises me. Somehow, we both could see all the potential in one another all along. Once our preoccupation with constant eating began to contract, our ability to self-actualize started to expand.

We still have the gamut of normal marital struggles. I think he will always be fastidiously tidy and my brain will always be on to the next thing before I've put my keys where they belong, or my folded laundry is put away. There are all the bills, chores and hassles of day-to-day life. We understand that it's typical to have significant differences about how to parent our young adult children. We know that marriage isn't supposed to be a cakewalk, even if you are being held up as a cute couple or marriage role models. The real difference is our sense of calm and coping that makes the everyday challenges small in comparison to how they used to be.

Over the summer of 2018, Ryan and I began to talk about this transformation we have been through. We looked back on all the weight gain and dysfunctional overeating, and we noted how intimately it was tied to the struggles we were having in our individual lives and in our marriage. Ultimately, we have been blessed with a great relationship. There has been a foundation of love and unconditional support unchanged from the evening at the Oakes Room in 2003 to this moment as we sit in a coffeehouse with our MacBooks almost touching. Our communication skills were poor, and our tendency to avoid problems allowed us to slip into terrible patterns, but we've learned that terrible patterns can be permanently broken.

It was easier to eat than talk. It was easier to eat than face our problems. It was easier to eat than get off the couch and go for a walk. Eating, it turned out, was the easiest and most destructive thing we could have done to cope with the stress of life. Fasting interrupted that ingrained pattern. With the noise and negativity of overeating out of the way, our collective strength and our ability to create an intentional life began shining through. That is how this book was born.

At this point, we look forward to the future for so many reasons. We have the energy to go out and do active things like hiking and swimming. We enjoy cooking and eating at home, thanks to the realization that fresh, simple food tastes far better than a chain restaurant meal covered in cheap oil and chemical-laden sauce. We have goals for our relationship and our family. Most importantly, running our Facebook support group has given us a unified sense of purpose around helping other people.

There is nothing more gratifying than hearing people say they felt inspired by our story, made some sort of tangible change in their own life and behavior, and now are seeing the positive results of those changes. In my friendship with Gin Stephens, she told me over and over what a dream come true it was to touch others' lives and now, thanks to her positive influence, we are experiencing a dream come true of our own.

My fears of perishing, of having no purpose once my kids were grown, were simply irrational and never came to fruition. I continue to work full-time as a medical scribe and though the job offers the same rewards it did four years ago, I feel a strong sense of calling to return to my counseling roots. There are moments when I am struck with a profound sense of having come completely full circle, looking all the way back at my early ambitions to be a teacher, counselor or helper of some kind.

Nothing lights me up like talking with people about the kind of life they have now and the ideal life they want to strive for. I have deemed my role with our IF group on Facebook as that of "Transformation Mentor", and I intend to expand that function formally in the near future. I like to say that counseling is in my training but encouraging is in my blood. My grandmother was the most naturally encouraging person I've ever known, and I know she would be so proud of my work to help others transform their lives.

We are now in full-on maintenance mode and refer to IF as our "forever lifestyle." Still, our bodies continue to change in gradual and subtle ways, and we plan to keep documenting the journey through photography. Our full before & after photo gallery is at our website, www.fastingfeastingfreedom.com. That's also where we have our blog, where we will post updates about updates about our lives and our future ventures. Thanks for reading our book. Please share it with others you think it may help. We want those struggling with obesity to believe there is a new life waiting for them and getting there doesn't have to involve deprivation or misery. We genuinely wish you all health, happiness, and a lifetime of food freedom.

-Ryan & Kim, "The Super Shrinking Smiths", October 2018

Ready to launch toward your own Unbelievable Freedom? Visit:
https://fastingfeastingfreedom.com/mentoring/
for more details about the Unbelievable Transformations Mentoring program.

Acknowledgements

We would like to thank our parents, Shelden, Rita, Eleanor, Lew, Peter, and Mary Ann, for all the values they instilled in us when we were growing up.

We would like to thank our children, Adam & Emma, for bringing us joy and being such bright lights during dark days.

We appreciate the time and attention of our earlier readers, Jeremy Lehan and Emma Gallimore, whose feedback helped us make the book better.

We thank Jeff Kirlin for taking the official after photo for our cover design.

Lastly, we are endlessly grateful to Gin Stephens for putting her story out into the world through *Delay, Don't Deny*, and for being an amazing mentor in both our story-writing and our work to positively impact the health journeys of others.

Made in the USA
Lexington, KY
01 April 2019